Acknowledgemen

Many, many thanks to the following for their encouragement, advice and enthusiasm regarding the writing and publication of Simply Behave.

Charlie Palmer – Educational Psychologist and Service Manager, Leicestershire.

Graham Falgate – Education Officer for Personal, Social and Health Education (PSHE) and Citizenship and Religious Education, Derby.

Janice Gunnell – SEAL co-ordinator, Sandwell.

John Pascoe – Project & Parent Support Worker, Carrick.

Linda Osborn – Head Teacher, Leicestershire.

Liz Williams – Primary Behaviour Consultant, Halton.

Rob Osborn – Anti Bullying Strategy Manager, Leicestershire.

Shally Saleri-Palmer – Primary Behaviour Specialist, Derby.

I am further indebted to the following for their in-depth analysis of Simply Behave. This included throwing their expertise, working knowledge of behaviour in schools, leadership and management skills in my direction. Gratefully received and caught!

Julie Bennett – Author of The Dyslexia Pocketbook, The Handwriting Pocketbook, Camel Study Skills: Improving memory, revision and exam techniques.

Julie spent weeks reading and rereading the text for content and grammatical accuracy.

Gill Denham - Head of Primary Phase, West London Academy.

For her willingness to implement many of the ideas outlined in Simply Behave. In addition, for her ability to look and see beyond the written word and see the opportunities for children and adults.

Mark Eales – Director for Education Standards, Doncaster Metropolitan Borough Council.

Mark, after reading the draft copy, not only volunteered to write a recommendation for Simply Behave, but had a significant input into the writing of the book. An incredible source of knowledge, encouragement and common sense.

BUT Finally!

Sue Sampson – My wife of forty years! Editor. Spell Checker. Nose to the grindstone keeper. Secretary. Encourager. Critical Friend. Reader. Rereader and re re reader.

Without doubt this book would never have reached the light of day if it hadn't been for Sue's belief in my ability to write it. Sue recognised the importance of such an undertaking because of the values, practice, principles and philosophies that walk through the pages of Simply Behave. From the very beginning of this three year venture Sue has had complete faith in the idea that Simply Behave will be an excellent additional resource in making schools a better place to be.

Thank you to you all. My third eye friends!

Published by GPWS Educational Consultancy
Copyright © Greg Sampson

Biography:

Greg Sampson enjoyed a long career in teaching, mainly in disadvantaged areas of Coventry. In 1997 he became headteacher of Sir Henry Parkes Primary School. During his career Greg took a particular interest in the practical ways to manage behaviour in the classroom and relate to challenging children. He has worked in hundreds of schools throughout the country, gathering expertise in a career spanning over 40 years. He enjoys opportunities to demonstrate behaviour strategies, good teaching techniques and positive leadership. This book, along with the suite of books about the R time (Relationships to Improve Education) programme is the practical outworking of Greg's many years of classroom and school based experience.

Greg is very happy to come into schools to demonstrate Simply Behave, discuss the methods used and provide training.

Want to know more?

Contact –

Greg Sampson
55, Garth Crescent
Binley
Coventry
CV3 2PP
Phone: 024 7665 9393
Mobile: 07946 333321
Email: gregsrtime@hotmail.com
Or explore the Simply Behave website at www.simplybehave.co.uk

Contents

Section 4 – Appendices

Thoughts for the day

Throughout the book there are 'thoughts for the day'. Where they have been taken from another source the author has been acknowledged.

All 'unacknowledged' quotes are
by Greg Sampson

Also throughout the book there are various items marked with this logo:

Schools may find it helpful to download these for their own use and to customise them - to have in the staff room, to display as posters around school, to put in brochures for staff and parents and to use as policy documents. These are all available as downloads on the Simply Behave website at www.simplybehave.co.uk

Foreword

> *Thought for the day*
>
> **If children come to us from strong, healthy and functioning families it makes our job a lot easier. If they do not come to us from strong, healthy and functioning families it makes our job more important.**
>
> *Barbara Colorose*

Sometimes working with challenging and, at times, unreceptive children can be soul destroying. However, when things begin to move in the right direction, night gives way to the dawn and the butterflies will emerge and start to fly.

The worst thing we can do as teachers is to leave a child without hope, to consign some of the children with whom we come into contact to a downward spiral of hopelessness. It is part of our professional responsibility to help them to realise they can rise above their circumstances and make a positive contribution not only to their own lives but to the lives of others.

To bring out the best in others we must bring out the best in ourselves. ***Simply Behave*** is a book that, at least, will make you think and challenge some of your ideas on behaviour management and, at best, breathe new life into the school.

It is a fact that almost two new teachers in every five leave the profession because they cannot manage the behaviour of some of the children they work with……..an alarming statistic. Of equal concern is the number of children who have their education blighted by others, making a mockery of the ideal of 'Education for All'! Education must be defined more by quality than availability.

Teachers can and will influence the climate they work in. They can be an inspiration as well as a source of hope and knowledge to the children in their direct care.

The following quote by Haim Ginott puts it far better than I can – but does it paint the whole picture?

'I have come to a frightening conclusion. I am the decisive element in the classroom. It is my personal approach that creates the climate. It is my daily mood that makes the weather. As a teacher I possess tremendous power to make a child's life miserable or joyous. I can be a tool of torture or an instrument of inspiration. I can humiliate or humour, hurt or heal. In all situations it is my response that decides whether crises will be escalated or de-escalated, and a child humanised or dehumanised.'

Dr. Haim Ginott 1922-1973.
A clinical psychologist, child therapist,
educator, and author of several books on
relationships.

Few would disagree with Dr. Ginott. There is no doubt that teachers have responsibility for creating the environment that promotes health, safety, inclusion, well being and learning. The aim of all teachers is to create a climate that is conducive to teaching and learning and it is the responsibility of all class based personnel to work together to achieve that goal.

However, I don't believe Dr. Ginott goes far enough in his statement. It is not only about adults influencing the class, for there are children who also have a massive impact on the climate of the classroom, and in some cases it can be a negative one! Just to clarify the point a little further. The sort of children I am referring to are those children whose absence brings about a certain peace! There will be children who can be so disruptive that their behaviour makes the lives of others at best frustrating and at worst totally unbearable.

It is imperative that such behaviour is managed and changed - but, children, like people of all ages, will only change their behaviour when it benefits them to do so.

I am confident that this book will give you simple, practical ideas and strategies to enable you to encourage children to change their behaviour because it not only benefits them but helps others too.

Simply behave, is about behaving not just for your sake but for others. Good behaviour must be exercised to maintain a healthy community. Once you believe that, it's simple!! Hence the title – **'Simply Behave'.**

Introduction:

> *Thought for the day*
>
> **Good behaviour must be exercised to maintain a healthy community.**

The purpose of this book is to take a fresh look at improving behaviour in and around schools. To give all those who work with children in Primary Schools the resources to support behaviour improvement; so that all school staff can work together, in a consistent way, to be part of an effective school.

It is designed to be a practical toolkit. It will not provide the reader with lots of theory. When all of the theory has been stripped away we arrive at what is really needed…..some simple, proven, easily implemented strategies that work…and which will enable children to **'Simply Behave'.**

Simply Behave is about creating the best possible school and classroom environment in which children can learn and teachers can teach.

Simply Behave will explore a range of situations, giving strategies and tools to deal with them, always keeping in mind the need to make these practical and simple.

Simply Behave says that it is vital that all adults working in schools become empowered workers - willing and able to set consistent, positive behavioural standards and at the same time provide warmth and support for the children.

Empowered workers can clearly and positively communicate their behavioural expectations to the children in their care, i.e. "I care too much about the children I work with to let them behave in a manner that is not in their best interests and the interests of the class and school".

In this age of inclusive education it is vital that we don't just make sure everyone is included but also **ensure that no one is left out** – and that applies to the adults in school as well as the children.

If you ask teachers the main purpose of their role I am certain the phrase, "To ensure the children reach their full potential", would be prominent. To enable children to grow and flourish effectively we need to create a 'fertile' environment. That fertile environment can be translated to the well coined phrase: **'The effective school'.**

In its simplest form an effective school is one where teachers are able to teach without disruption and the children are able to learn in a secure and safe environment. However, if those are the two major outcomes of an effective school what is the infrastructure that needs to be in place to ensure that happens? What are the essential ingredients that enable a school to thrive and become a very good school?

Although there isn't a magic formula I would suggest there are certain things that need to be in place if the school is to be successful for all of its stakeholders. One of the privileges of my work is travelling around schools, working with the whole school community. I have been to many wonderful schools and I've come to the conclusion that the following seven aspects, all inter-related and of equal importance, create a school that everyone can be proud of:

1) **R**eal leadership.

2) **R**ichness of teaching.

3) **R**elationships that are positive and inclusive.

4) **R**elevant curriculum.

5) **R**eflective of the views of others.

6) **R**espect for everything and everyone.

7) **R**obust discipline policy.

These are the seven **Rs**, the rich soil that schools can provide to ensure healthy and consistent growth.

Simply Behave is divided into the following sections:

- **Section One** explores creating the environment for behaviour improvement. This section explores the important aspects of a framework that will create confidence, for all involved, and a desire to move forward together, seeking further growth and well being.

- **Section Two** is about Behaviour Improvement – planning to practice. Good behaviour has its roots firmly established in good teaching, good classroom management and good school management. For a school to stand still is not an option. To ensure and enable further progress to be maintained agreed processes need to be in place, and used, to enable the school to move forward. Behaviour improvement is one such process. This section will start by looking at the 'now' and move on to developing and implementing plans to ensure continuous improvement.

- **Sections Three** looks at specific measures for specific circumstances.

- **Section Four** is the appendices containing simplified policy documents as well as expanded explanations of some issues referred to in the main body of the book.

Section One

Creating the Environment for Behaviour Improvement.

> *Thought for the day*
> **Behaviour starts with a 'B'. If only it started with a 'Me'!**

Real Leadership

> *Thought for the day*
>
> **A leader takes people where they want to go. A great leader takes people where they don't necessarily want to go, but ought to be.**
>
> *Rosalynn Carter*
> *Former first lady of the United States*

Put simply, behaviour management starts at the top and needs to be led by the Headteacher – the Behaviour Manager. The degree of importance that the Head places on behaviour, and the way that they lead on this aspect, will have a fundamental impact on the success, or otherwise, of behaviour management across the whole school. The Head must lead from the front, support all other co-behaviour managers, and fully take on board their own role and responsibility in the school's behaviour strategy, for it to succeed. Leadership is the prime function of the Headteacher. Interestingly if we scramble the letters of Leadership we get the phrase 'Heads Peril'. It can be a perilous occupation at times but when things go right the 'peril' becomes a 'pearl'! For any leader to be successful it is important to bear in mind the following four things:

1) Role - The **role** of a leader is to **create followers.**

2) Task - The **task** of a leader is to **bring about** constructive and necessary **change.**

3) Responsibility - The **responsibility** of a leader is to bring about change in a way that is **responsive to the real and long-term needs of the school** and its stakeholders.

4) Source of power of a leader - The greatest **source of power** available to a leader is the **trust and loyalty** that others place in the leader and their leadership. It is also important that the headteacher demonstrates trust and loyalty towards others.

What are the necessary ingredients to enable the Head to carry out their crucial role as effectively as possible? Five actions to SHARE that are key for an effective leader carrying out their role:

- **S - Share a vision:** Effective leaders possess and communicate a picture of their goals to others.

- **H - Help Implement strategy:** Effective leaders understand and implement steps towards reaching the goals.

- **A - Ability to delegate tasks:** Effective leaders recognise that it is impossible to do it all themselves! They delegate.

- **R - Respect others.** Effective leaders value what others do, when they do it and in the way they do it – and they tell them!!

- **E - Empower people:** Effective leaders mobilise and equip people to join them in the cause.

• **Share a vision:**

An effective leader will possess a clear vision of where to go, as well as being able to communicate this to the rest of the team, in a way that wins their trust and confidence.

A visionary Headteacher enables others to feel they have a real stake and say in the project. They empower people to experience the vision as if it is their own.

Effective leaders thrive on change enabling them to draw the new boundaries change brings about. The ability to communicate with people at all levels is a crucial leadership skill. However, one of the most important things a leader must remember is that their actions, and not just words, set the example for the whole staff team.

Leadership calls for clear communication about expectations, goals, responsibility, performance and evaluation.

Effective leaders lead with enthusiasm, with a bounce in their step, and with a 'can-do attitude'. Enthusiasm is contagious and it is nearly always worth catching!

Thoughts for the day

Leadership is the art of getting others to do something you want done because they want to do it.

Dwight D. Eisenhower
34th President of the United States. 1953 – 1961

A leader is best when people barely know they exist. When their work is done, they will say: we did it ourselves.

Lao Tzu
A 6th century B.C. Chinese philosopher. Generally recognised as the Father of Taoism.

• **Help implement strategy:**

In the implementation of a strategy there are three key aspects:

1) The starting point   2) The route   3) The goal

The starting point: the issues that are to be addressed must be clearly identified and communicated to the appropriate people.

The route: this is the process involved in ensuring the particular issues have every chance to arrive at the successful solution.

The goal: this is the successful completion of the process with the associated rewards.

What does this mean in practice? In terms of improving behaviour in the school, implementing the strategy could look something like this:

1) The starting point: 'The issue is that there is a concern that the behaviour in the school does not fully support teaching and learning, identified by indicators such as the following':

1. Four temporary exclusions for behaviour this term.
2. Several complaints from parents regarding bullying incidents.
3. The school council bringing concerns about behaviour at break times.
4. A general recognition from staff that behaviour is not good.
5. Teachers find some classes too challenging to teach effectively.
6. Ofsted, in their most recent inspection, highlighted poor behaviour as a cause for concern.

2) The route:
1. Carry out a behaviour audit as outlined on *pages 41-49*.
2. Adopt the Rules, Rewards and Repercussions recommended by 'Simply Behave'.
3. An emphasis is placed on classroom management and classroom practice using guidance from 'Simply Behave', as well as existing practice.
4. A meeting/letter is sent to parents outlining the new system and how they can support the school and their children.
5. A review of the new regime is carried out within a term of implementation.

3) The goal: Clear evidence that behaviour has improved, demonstrated by:

1. A reduction in exclusions.
2. A general sense of well being in and around the school.
3. Positive feedback from stakeholders in the school.
4. A 'clean bill of health' from Ofsted when the school is revisited.
5. The behaviour audit carried out again with positive outcomes.

• Ability to delegate tasks:

The need for successful delegation is essential if everyone is to be involved in the process and share in the celebrations of achieving successful outcomes.

Delegation isn't about relinquishing authority but allowing others to make decisions that will enhance and prosper the process. This involves three key elements:

1. Communicating what the 'leader' wants and is needed.
2. Conveying how and when to do it.
3. Being given the authority to achieve it.

• **Respect others:**

Respect is a vital element in the relationship between a leader and their team. In fact it is an essential ingredient of a successful team. You demonstrate your trust, loyalty and respect for others through your actions – how much you check and control the work of others. How much you delegate and how much you allow people to participate.

Individuals who are unable to respect and trust others often fail as leaders, becoming at best micro managers and at worst ending up doing all the work themselves!

Lead like you trust your team.

Lead by giving them solid directions from the beginning.

Communicate with them clearly and consistently along the way and don't be frightened to step back!

Create an atmosphere of support and belonging, ensuring that no one feels left out.

• **Empower people:**

The key to empowerment is having a clear vision that is communicated so people know what the end result looks like. Everyone is working together in delivering the same objective.

Along the route there will be times we have to ad lib, agree to differ, but there is that desire to work together as a unit, a team.

Empowerment is a powerful feeling. It means you truly give others the power to deliver the objective, not because you dispense it, but because they take the responsibility.

Thought for the day

The beauty of empowering others is that your own power is not diminished in the process.

Barbara Colorose.

Richness of Teaching
– or the qualities of a successful 'teacher'

Thought for the day

To bring out the best in your pupils you need to bring out the best in yourself.

Let's not beat about the bush! Some teachers are better at teaching than others!

Let us not fool ourselves with the idea that all teachers are the same in terms of their effectiveness as teachers. There are very few naturally gifted teachers; most of us have to learn our craft. It is important that we recognise excellent teachers and use them and their skills for the benefit of the whole school. It is unhelpful to think that if we recognise excellence we also are in danger of highlighting the not excellent. What we are in fact trying to do is to help all of us to improve the way we work in our schools. There needs to be the realisation that many of the skills that an excellent teacher has can be taught and therefore caught by others, helping us all to become more effective teachers.

What makes effective teachers? It is about creating in the children a desire to learn – and to enable their class to be effective, the teacher has to be effective.

What are the skills and qualities that contribute to making the effective teacher? In my experience of working with thousands of children across the age ranges, and observing hundreds of teachers, I have discovered the following criteria which I've placed under three headings:

Quality teachers as people. Summary - They are not playing a role, they are real people who show their humanity and, as people, they are approachable.

Quality teachers as professionals. Summary - As professionals they are respectful of the needs of the pupils they work with and for.

Quality teachers as role models. Summary - As role models they set positive examples that are challenging, desirable as well as attainable.

Quality teachers as people:

- **They are fair.**

  One criticism you constantly hear regarding authority of any description are the words, "It's not fair". The majority of children will accept 'advice' from authority providing it is given fairly, with consideration for all.

- **They listen and are people you can talk to.**

  To listen to a child isn't just about being attentive; it is about hearing what is said and responding in the appropriate way at the right time. This often requires patience as well as empathy.

- **They can have a laugh but they also can keep order.**

  The vast majority of children want to feel safe in school. That safety comes from knowing that the 'teacher' is in control. However, being in charge can only be effective when firm control is tempered with knowing smiles.

- **They don't shout and they don't go on.**

  The raising of one's voice becomes extremely effective when it is an unusual occurrence. This short, sharp, shock treatment usually has the desired effect. There is a great deal of truth behind the old adage, 'Quiet teacher, quiet class'.

  When something is going on and on, without a pause, someone will eventually switch it off. When someone goes on and on at a child, it will have little effect apart from creating the desire in the child, as well as others, to switch off.

- **They will admit that they make mistakes.**

  Learning is a complex process but there is no doubt learning from mistakes is part of that process. In an environment where pupils are concerned about making mistakes, it can restrict learning opportunities if not handled well. What a wonderful example a teacher can make by demonstrating to their pupils that making mistakes is an integral part of learning as well as life.

- **They have the ability to make you feel good.**

  What a gift it is to make someone feel good! The glow factor can last an eternity; as can making someone feel 'small'. Let's make sure the children in our care not only know they can please us, but can recognise when they have done so and how they have done so!

  Creating positive relationships in the classroom will almost certainly establish an atmosphere in which respect, care and achievement flourish.

- **They get to know 'their' children as individuals.**

  Good teachers get to know their children. They know about their families and some of the challenges that they face. Knowing a little about what makes each child tick helps to develop the kind of relationships on which success in all areas of the child's life at school can be founded.

Quality teachers as professionals:

- **They have a good knowledge of the subjects they teach.**

  There is much truth in the statement, 'A little knowledge is dangerous'. The children in our care expect teachers to have good subject knowledge – please don't disappoint them. There is nothing more frustrating than attending a course where you come away having learnt very little because the course facilitator hasn't got enough knowledge to inspire you as the learner.

- **They can communicate that knowledge effectively and with interest.**

  'You can lead a horse to water but you can't make it drink'! Unless you salt its oats!!

  As educators we are in the business of salting oats, making the facts and knowledge we are required to share as interesting, palatable and desirable as possible.

  Every effort should be made to stimulate the children to want to learn with a relevant and perceptive approach.

- **They vary the ways they teach, embracing different learning styles.**

  There are three main modes of learning: Visual, Auditory and Kinaesthetic (Seeing, Hearing and Doing). It is very important that when planning what we are teaching we consider these different learning styles – especially as individual children will relate to different styles.

  The methods chosen need to be well matched to the particular focus and demand of the lesson. It is vital that there is a clear emphasis on making the most productive use of the time available to both children and teachers.

- **They work hard as well as work 'smart'.**

  There is no doubting that teaching is a very challenging profession. For teachers to give of their best they not only have to work hard but ensure, more importantly, they don't wear themselves out. Using their time and energies in the most productive way should be a consideration at all times.

- **They treat pupils as individuals.**

  Every Child Matters. This isn't about creating individual work programmes for every child. It is about ensuring that every individual child feels valued. I have found that two of the best and simplest ways of doing this are:

  1) To use the pupil's given name as often as possible both verbally and in the written form (e.g. when making written comments on work).

  2) To know what works for the child and then taking every opportunity to give appropriate praise as well as relevant 'encouragement'.

- **They encourage an input from pupils as part of the learning process.**

  "Children should be seen and not heard", is a saying that should be dead and buried. It is vital that children have a say in their learning as well as in their learning process.

  Their views need to be weighed and considered. They should be consulted about the learning input as well as the learning outcomes.

  A significant approach in this aspect of learning is the use of challenging questions. Good questioning needs to consider three important aspects:

  1) The need to consider what the children already know.

  2) The need to extend what the children require or desire to know and

  3) The need to verify that the children have understood.

- **They have a philosophy that can be easily identified by the way they work and care.**

  Children must know that the teachers they work with have a philosophy that basically says, 'We care enough about you to ensure that you have the best possible chances to grow and prosper'.

- **They have an inclusive approach to the educational process.**

  Inclusive education is not about making sure everyone is included but trying to make sure no one is left out! Hopefully, you will have experienced the awe that comes through the speaker who, when talking to the assembled masses, is able to create the feeling that the talk is directed not just towards us, but is about us! Whatever senses are aroused in us we certainly feel involved. It is that involvement a good teacher not only creates but uses positively for the benefit of others.

- **Their use of resources is both thoughtful and imaginative.**

  Using resources should be part and parcel of the tools of the trade. However, whichever resources a teacher might turn to, they need to be used intelligently as well as imaginatively and creatively. This will, in turn, make creative demands on the children, encouraging them to want to learn as well as helping them to extend their learning.

- **They set fair processes in place that are known and agreed by all.**

  For example, **noise levels** in the classroom aren't about volume but about the appropriateness of the noise level to the activity the children are carrying out. 'Quiet Reading' will have a lower tolerance level to noise than, for instance, children working in groups debating an issue.

  What is important is that the noise level is agreed by all and that should be adhered to by everyone in the class. In Key Stage Two I have found it very helpful to categorise the noise levels in terms of centimetres. For example 'We will be using for the next 15minutes 30cm voices. I will be using a 4m voice because I need to be heard at the back of the classroom'.

  In Key Stage One and Foundation it is helpful to categorise sound level in terms of levels of whispers, for example quiet, medium or loud.

  The definition and volume associated by this description should be clearly defined and known by the children. The voice of the teacher should nearly always be a 'little' louder than that used by the children because of the requirement to reach the whole of the class. The children themselves can agree the noise levels and as they adhere to them there should be some recognition for their efforts – hence the quiet time barometer on the wall or their tables/desks.

  In addition to appropriate noise levels the children must be familiar with the **'know levels'**- in other words what they can and cannot do whilst in school.

  For example: 'I **know** I must put my hand up to ask a question of the teacher.'

  'I **know** I need to get permission to go to the toilet.'

Quality teachers as role models:

- **They model the behaviour that they want - do as I do.**

  One of the key ways children learn is by imitating others. Not only is it important that the rules are known but that those in authority demonstrate them, as well. This not only underlines the rules as a learning example but also emphasises their importance.

- **They demonstrate on a regular basis that they enjoy being in school.**

  This is not about wearing a false smile but bringing real smiles to others by what you say, by what you do, as well as about who you are.

- **They don't give up on you.**

  There are those children who will give up on themselves even if they don't recognise they are doing so. It is vital that by your positive attitude towards them you are clearly demonstrating that you value them.

- **They are respectful of all the children and adults.**

  It is often too easy to be dismissive of people without really taking the time to get to know them and the circumstances they find themselves in. Judging a book by its cover can be a common occurrence in our quick fix society. Judging children by their reputation, or cover, will never replace the good old fashioned process made famous in the song, 'Getting to know you'. Giving the children time is one of the best gifts we can give them. Time invested wisely will not go unrewarded and will make the world of difference for all concerned.

- **They set sensible standards of dress and manners.**

  This is not just about the appropriate clothes we wear but the smiles we have as well. As children learn by imitation – give them something positive to imitate.

- **They give praise much more than punishment.**

  Any discipline programme worth its salt should be about a 'process for praise and not a procedure for punishment'. Punishments will almost certainly underline what a child has done wrong; praise will underline what is to be aspired to and create an understanding of what is right.

- **They clearly demonstrate they enjoy being with the pupils by the things they say and do.**

  Joy is not influenced by things from without but by the things from within. It can be argued that real joy comes from doing something really worthwhile, engaging in it fully, not just for your benefit but for others.

- **They are ambitious for themselves as well as their pupils.**

  As workers with children we need to foster a healthy ambition within the children in our care. Not a driving, destructive sort of ambition based upon unrealistic expectations, but an ambition with its roots firmly based in doing our best for the child. This approach is more effective in enabling the child to do, and become, the best they can.

- **They don't use sarcasm.**

  Sarcasm is saying the opposite of what you really mean, often as a way of being funny. The trouble is that the majority of children don't understand sarcasm and it can be very hurtful. As workers with children we should never use anything that can be harmful to children whether, physically, emotionally, psychologically or intellectually.

- **They apologise when they make a mistake.**

  The action of saying sorry not only begins to create trust but can help to establish a positive relationship – particularly if the sorry is meant, and accepted. Saying sorry is not a weakness; it is a strength that needs to be experienced by the giver as well as the recipient. As I have already stated, saying sorry is not just about using the word, it demands action.

· **They keep on top of their emotions and 'keep their cool'.**

There is clear evidence that some children get a sense of enjoyment from the 'teacher' losing their cool. It is also true that for some children it can be quite a frightening experience. As for the teacher it can lead to a sense of regret. Whatever the range of emotions felt and experienced 'losing control' is a no-win situation.

· **They respect the children as people.**

A balanced approach when working with, and for, children is essential. Getting to know a child and how they learn and communicate will serve to improve opportunities for learning. Getting to know a child doesn't happen by accident it needs to be a conscious effort by the teacher to come alongside the child to enable teaching to be more effective. On *page 28* I've listed some ways for you to consider in developing an effective and constructive relationship with a child.

T.E.A.C.H.

Although it is important to develop positive relationships with the individual children in your care it is also essential to have a positive relationship with the whole class of children you have to manage. The management of the many will help you to manage any. The key to good classroom management is firstly to recognise it is complex and differs from class to class; it is also hard work. Being aware of these complexities, as well as the work involved, is as important as the ability to unravel them. It is essential to identify the key features that must be in place so the class can work successfully. Below are five simple tips that may help in identifying as well as confirming ways to be a successful classroom manager and practitioner. I've used the acronym TEACH as an aide memoir.

T. E. A. C. H.
Try to remember these 5 'simple' tips

T is for time. Ensure you start on time and the pace of the lesson is appropriate for the content as well as the children.

E is for environment. Ensure your room is set out appropriately.

A is for apparatus. Ensure the resources are at hand, planned and well presented.

C is for control. Ensure the children know the rules and instructions associated with the lesson.

H is for help. Ensure you make the best use of support staff and other available help.

T is for time:

Three important aspects in the area of **time:**

*   The timing of the lesson,

*   The pace of the lesson,

*   And minimising disruption to the 'flow' of the lesson.

The timing of the lesson:

Key: Start and finish whatever you are doing in the given times: For example registration begins at 9am and should finish 6 minutes later. Literacy is timetabled for one hour, beginning at 9.20 and concluding at 10.20.

The pace of the lesson:

Key: One of the key motivating factors is to finish what is started. A lesson must be designed to have a beginning, middle and an end. Timing is essential, ensuring goals are reached and content covered. It is better to finish early than allow the lesson to drag on to an inconclusive conclusion. We may not create a class of Masterminds – but the activity should be designed to enable children to say, 'I've started, so I will finish'!!

Minimising disruption:

Key: It is important that the organisation of the school is such that interruptions to lessons are kept to the necessary minimum. There is nothing worse for a teacher than having settled the class an unnecessary interruption occurs – a message, a late child's arrival, a parent, a colleague, a visitor from the LEA. Although all these visits are necessary there is a time and place for each of them.

Messages: (unless very urgent) should be given to the teacher during a natural break so the teacher can decide when and how to deliver the message.

If space permits, placing a notice board outside the classroom where notices could be posted is another idea worthly of consideration.

Late children: (if this happens regularly then the school needs to look at their attendance and lateness policy). When late children arrive they should enter the teaching area with little or no disruption to the class.

Parents: Only in extreme circumstances should a parent visit a classroom to see a teacher during school time. Usually, if parents request to see a teacher then it must be at a mutually agreed time and with the knowledge of the Headteacher.

Colleague: Any internal visitors must be very considerate about when, why and how they contact the class teacher. Very rarely is it essential to interrupt when the teacher is in the act of direct supervision of their class of children.

A visitor from the Local Authority: All visitors should make an appointment through the prescribed channels. If it is to 'observe' a teacher, when working, then the purpose and timing of the 'visit' should be known and adhered to by both parties.

Much of the above is common sense as well as good manners, but in my experience the flow and pace of the lesson can and will be disrupted by thoughtless and unnecessary interruptions.

E is for Environment:

This aspect of T.E.A.C.H. embraces both the physical environment as well as the ethos. To do everything that follows is hard work – but you will find it is certainly well worth the effort.

The physical environment:

Key: Put very simply, clutter in the room will quickly become clatter, accidents waiting to happen. Inevitably that will lead to chatter (unwanted noise) and this will certainly shatter an environment that is conducive to safety, teaching and learning. The way the classroom is set out is vital. From the positioning of desks /tables to the thoughtful variety of displays. From the appropriate and considered seating arrangements to the placement of shelving and cabinets.

Whatever the arrangements you make, the key issue is that everyone is able to breathe freely in the room. By that I mean there is ample space for effective movement around the teaching area. Get that right and the other things will not fall, instead everything will fall into place!!

Are all those drawers necessary?
Are the spare tables helping or hindering?
Do we really need all those coats and bags in the room?
Is the teacher's desk in the right place?
Is the teacher's desk necessary?
Is there room for a carpet area?
Is the carpet area appropriate in size and position?
Are the resources easily accessible?
Can better use be made of the floor space?
Is the classroom pupil and people friendly?

The ethos:

Key: Is the teacher able to teach effectively and the children learn constructively?

One of the recurring questions in an interview for a teaching job is, 'If I walked into your classroom what would you expect me to see?'

The answer in a nutshell, 'A classroom that enables learning to take place positively, productively and with purpose and praise'. This is all about how the children learn and the teacher teaches.

Is there a sense of excitement?
Are the children cooperating?
Is there an atmosphere of care and compassion?
Are relationships good and clearly positive in the classroom?
Is it a classroom that you would like your own children to be taught in?

If all the answers to these questions are a resounding YES then you can guarantee that the ethos of the room is not created by accident but by the teacher putting into place initiatives that create a positive learning environment.

PSHCE would be high on the agenda through a range of activities like SEAL, R time, Circle Time, Talk partners, Buddy Systems, commitment to children's participation as members of class and school council.

 The objective is not to ensure that everyone is friends but there is, in the classroom, a friendly environment where this phrase makes sense: "Thank you for creating a classroom where I've got friends I don't even like!!"

A is for apparatus:

Good quality, appropriate and accessible resources are essential to enhancing learning - from sharpened pencils, to the more sophisticated use and availability of electronic equipment. There is nothing worse than not having the correct tools for the job. It can lead to frustration and poor outcomes.

The sharing of resources is important, as well as necessary, BUT if the sharing hinders the progress of the children then reconsider the use of the equipment. For example a text book in Numeracy that could create the problem for children working together because the children are working from different pages. At best this is inconvenient and at worse creates the potential for going off task and arguing.

When apparatus is required is it available readily and with ease?

Are the children expected to get the apparatus or is it ready and in place for them to use? Much will depend on the time and sort of equipment required but there must be a considered approach to its use. The key being, will the use of the apparatus add to the How, When, What and Why the children learn?

Valued resources will bring about a valued response both in their use and the care with which they are used.

C is for Control:

This issue revolves around the three R's - 'Rules', 'Rewards' and 'Repercussions of not following the rules'. Please see Section Two of the book which is directly related to these three topics.

H is for Help:

Thought for the day

It is amazing how much you can accomplish when it doesn't matter who gets the credit.

Harry S Truman
33rd President of the United States. 1884-1972

Asking for help is a professional strength. If you need it you should ask for it. Wherever we are on the ladder of the teaching profession we all need help at times.

How can you, then, maximise the valuable contribution of all of the additional support staff available to you? This could involve a variety of people who are regularly with you in the classroom – Teaching Assistants, Learning Mentors, Transition Mentors, SENCO, Non-teaching support staff, parents, older pupils and so on.

There will be other occasional support staff that could include student teachers, Local Authority representatives, Supply Teachers, Dining Room Support staff, Specialist teachers, Guest visitors as well as Specialist support staff.

All have a vital role to play and the class teacher has a key role in managing their involvement. All should be seen as very much part of the broader based teaching team. It is important that none of them are thrown in at the deep end and that they are supported in their role of helping you, working with your children.

If the potential for disruptive behaviour is an issue then knowledge of the 3 R's (**R**ules, **R**ewards and **R**epercussions) is vital.

If the class is very able then the work given them needs to be challenging as well as interesting.

If the classroom relationships are demanding then make sure the demands are known.

It is as important to share management strategies as well as content of the lessons, with all helpers.

To enable them to work effectively, as well as supportively, it is essential that when it comes to managing the class there is a common purpose, allied to a common approach:

> 1) *By that I mean their roles must be clearly identified and understood and*

> 2) *By using the same management processes used by the resident class teacher - the three R's as well as the same routines outlined in T.E.A.C.H.*

Volunteers from amongst the parents might become involved in the school in helping to teach the basics. Selected parents may be involved in the family aspect of the SEAL programme as a way of helping the parents with their child's education both in and out of school. Homework club could have the facility to involve parents. Parents could be asked to sit in on lessons with their child as a way of supporting both the child and the teacher.

Relationships

Thought for the day

We control fifty percent of a relationship. We influence one hundred percent of it.

Barbara Colorose

Relationships are the building blocks of society. Being in positive relationships transforms the way we see the world and transforms our ability to succeed within it.

Yet, learning about how to be in relationship with others can be very hit and miss. If we believe that forming positive relationships is important then there is the need to acquire the skills necessary to establish positive relationships.

We all recognise the importance of teaching the basics in other subject areas and there are many children who need to be taught the basic skills of communicating and relating effectively. Through relationships we can thrive and our sense of well-being is high. Without relationships we can be literally lost and alone. Sadly in our modern society there can be too great an emphasis on **I** and not **We**.

Many T.V. programmes focus on the breakdown of relationships instead of the building of them. Too much emphasis is placed upon competition instead of valuing and celebrating differences. Reality T.V. becomes compulsive viewing when things explode or get out of hand.

Emphasising good manners, co-operation and respect should be taught as well as caught by children at home and in school. However, there are those who take longer to develop the skills, as well as those who are not taught, or have little or no opportunity to observe them in practice. Just as we teach children academic skills, social qualities need to be treated and valued in a similar way.

In school, where we aim to encourage the children to value the positives we can be going against the tide of modern society – no wonder there are many who would say that teaching is the hardest job in the world. We need others 'on-side' which is why, later in this book, the importance of involving the whole family in the Behaviour Improvement Plan is stressed, and not just the individual children.

Over the years I have come to realise the following:
*   When a school puts positive relationships high on the agenda the outcomes will always prove beneficial for all in the school community.

- Good teachers seem to always have good children or is it they have the ability to make children good!?

- Positive relationships are at the heart of all that is good in the school context.

- When relationships are supportive and positive then we can really 'learn to fly 'and embrace personal development.

- Relationships that encourage growth, and foster openness and honesty, will lead to progress and achievement.

- Relationships that value others will raise self esteem.

- Relationships that endeavour to understand will bring about empathy.

- Relationships that grow and foster team spirit will bring about inclusiveness.

Beware!

- Relationships have the capacity to work for us or against us!

- When relationships are fragile and negative then we not only stumble at obstacles we can waste a good deal of our time looking for them.

- Relationships are much more than mere words. Words without the accompanying actions are not only empty and hollow, but also damaging. The talk must be supported by the walk.

Most important words:

The six most important words:
'I admit that I was wrong.'

The five most important words:
'You did a great job'.

The four most important words:
'What do you think?'

The three most important words:
'May I help?'

The two most important words:
'Thank you'.

The most important word:
'We'.

The least important word:
'I'.

By Shane K Anderson

Where do we learn how to form positive relationships?

In the home – but a third of marriages end in divorce and that can bring with it very real challenges for children and adults alike. There will be children who witness domestic abuse within the family and the healing process can be long and painful. More and more children are growing up in families where positive relationship modelling is not always available.

In school – but where does this fit into the curriculum? Is it just squeezed into an occasional PSHCE slot? Children and young people often act out what they see at home and on T.V. and these can be a mixture of positive and negative experiences.

Amongst our peers – this can often rely more on good fortune than judgement, depending on who is in our peer group.

Realising that it is vital to have positive relationships not just in school but within the classroom I developed a programme called **R time** – a programme that focuses on the building and modelling of relationships between children.

R time enables children to get to know all of the other children in their class – not just the ones that they would usually choose to.

R time is a very practical programme which enables children to develop the social and emotional skills required for a fulfilled, confident and contented life.

It provides a vehicle for children to experience the Social and Emotional Aspects of Learning and has been recognised nationally as an excellent support to the Primary National Strategy programme known as S.E.A.L.

For more information about R time *See Appendix 5, Page 167.*

Thought for the day

Relationships that cross boundaries will not only build bridges but enable us to cross them.

Creating positive relationships with children

Let's build bridges rather than dig ditches; after all the view is much better!

- Greet your children individually, by name, when they come into your classroom.

- Stop and chat with them in other areas of the school.

- Make a point of initiating conversation.

- Monitor and modify your tone and body language to show an openness and friendly concern.

- Show interest and try and give complete attention when the children are talking to you.

- Show care, concern and empathy.

- Smile and show a sense of humour.

- Find out as much as you can about the children's likes and dislikes.

- Bring up non-academic topics of mutual interest.

- Say something positive to the children at the end of the day.

- Offer to shake their hands as they leave to go home.

- Focus on their strengths.

- Remind the children about things they have done well.

- Give them responsibilities in the class.

- Keep their parents informed – especially about the good things.

- Make it your goal to establish positive relationships with even the most difficult children.

Relevant Curriculum

Thought for the day

We may not have a class of high flyers but our aim must be to help the children fly as high as they can.

Our desire is not just to create learners but <u>lovers of learning</u>. This entails being fully aware of the needs of the children and treating them accordingly. Teaching methods and styles vary not just from school to school but from class to class. Methods, whatever they are, need to be appropriate for the teacher and the children they are teaching.

When identifying a relevant and realistic curriculum for our children who better to consult than the children themselves? In a nation wide survey children said that there were five key **outcomes** to well-being in childhood as well as later life, not only to put a smile on their faces but to influence their whole view of school and life in general.

B – Be healthy.
E – Enjoy and Achieve.
A – Achieve economic well-being.
M – Make a positive contribution.
S – Stay safe.

These have been adopted by the government as the key outcomes, described in detail in Every Child Matters: Change for Children - the government's programme aimed at transforming children's services.

The way the curriculum is organised needs to reflect those five outcomes, and the **Inputs** should enable these **Outcomes** to be addressed.

Being Healthy: Physically, mentally and emotionally healthy children and young people. This must include the encouragement of parents, carers and families to promote healthy choices.

Enjoy and achieve: The need to be ready for school. To attend regularly and enjoy school. To achieve personal and social development and enjoy recreation. To do the best they can and achieve realistic educational standards for themselves. For the parents, carers and families to recognise they must make every effort to support learning.

Achieve economic well-being: To recognise that education is not only beneficial for the now but the future – enabling children to consider further education as a realistic option. To be ready for employment when leaving full time education. To live in households free from a low income.
For parents, carers and families to be supported and to be economically active.

Make a positive contribution: For children and young people to engage in law – abiding and positive behaviour in and out of school. Develop positive relationships. Develop self confidence and successfully deal with the changes and challenges of everyday life. Make right choices. For the Parents, carers and families to promote positive behaviour.

Stay Safe: For children and young people to stay safe from bullying and discrimination. Safe from maltreatment, neglect, violence and sexual exploitation. Safe from crime and anti-social behaviour in and out of school. Having security, stability and are cared for. For parents, carers and families to provide safe homes and stability.

Not only is it invaluable to consult children it is also essential to consult those who have invested heavily in the education system by devoting their lives to teaching children. Teachers make up a large percentage of that category. Teachers have the central responsibility to provide the children in our schools with the dignity of becoming literate and numerate. This is the challenge for all of us and the vast majority of our primary schools are achieving this vital aim.

However, there are schools that fall short of that essential target and therein lays the challenge. Do we throw more Literacy and Numeracy lessons at the children hoping that more of the same will eventually conquer? Or do we look for other routes, the 'routes of relevance'? Let's broaden the opportunities for the children, in the context of the primary curriculum, using integrated studies, first hand experiences, local interests and child-initiated ideas that embrace Literacy and Numeracy. These used creatively can sow the seeds of success for those children for whom success doesn't come easily.

Reflective of the Views of Others

Thought for the day

The whole purpose of education is to turn mirrors into windows.

Sydney J Harris
American journalist. Born 1917 – died 1986

Is the school you work in an island surrounded by sea and difficult to reach? Or a community that everyone feels part of? At its best a school is the heart of a community, being fully integrated into the community it serves.

New school buildings are arising everywhere. Schools are arriving in the 21st century - and about time too! Children, parents, governors and staff are being offered opportunities to become actively involved in the design of schools that are fit for purpose – and in the decisions about what takes place within them. Solar panels, wide corridors, purpose built, light and bright dining areas. Discrete yet open classrooms. Cloakrooms that miraculously hold all the coats. I.T. suites that have enough room for children as well as the computers. Smaller playing fields, but playgrounds that can accommodate all the children. A hall that isn't a squeeze. Community spaces for out-of-school-hours' activities. A library that gives the books the status they deserve. Staffrooms that go a long way to match the sort of environment some 'white collar' workers have been used to. Functional offices for the admin staff that tick most of the right boxes.

Schools are changing all the time and as the living bricks that make up the school come and go, so the climate and ethos of the school ebbs and flows - not defined by bricks and mortar but by its pupils, parents, governors and staff.

Schools need to engage in dialogue and capture the imagination of the communities they serve – raise questions and be prepared to answer them. Be aware of community issues and act as full partners, using education and opportunities in school to address these. Does your school look outward and see the benefits of so doing, or are you an inward facing exclusive school community? Only by harnessing the wealth of resources and experience of others can the school truly thrive and be a community school in more than just name.

In the late nineties schools had the opportunity to designate themselves as **community schools**. At the time I remember being concerned about the extra work load this might involve. My mind jumped to fetes, family discos, after school activities for the community, car boot sales, open days, garden parties etc. Now, in the 21st century we have the designated title and role of, 'Extended Schools'. The underlying feature of both Community and Extended Schools should not just be about what they do and how effectively they do it but how successful the schools are with communication in the community. Perhaps it would be more helpful to label the school a **Communication school** rather than a **Community school**. The effective **action** of a community school is good communication between the school and all its stakeholders.

How might this communication work in practice?
There are five basic ingredients for effective communication:

Informing, Liaising, Consulting, Negotiating and Evaluating.

It is not always necessary to use all five parts. Much will depend on the information to be imparted as well as the recipients of the information. What is important, however, is to have some degree of regard for the skills, strategies and ways of communicating outlined above.

To help clarify the use of these processes I've used five examples where all or selected aspects of the above will be required:

Informing: (To give out facts or information) - Information regarding school holiday dates or an increase in the cost of the school dinners.

Liaising: (To arrange something of mutual benefit) – Liaising with a parent regarding a meeting to discuss an issue about their child.

Consulting: (To seek advice, views or information) – The school has decided to do a behaviour audit and as part of the process relevant stakeholders are consulted about current practice.

Negotiating: (By discussion seeking an agreement) – The school would like to adjust the school hours. The governors could be presented with a paper outlining the new proposals.

Evaluating: (Judging the worth of something) – To help improve punctuality of the children the classrooms are opened and supervised at 8.45. After a trial period of one month figures of punctuality are compared before and after the new arrangements.

Within the examples outlined above there will be a crossing of the boundaries between the communication skills. What is important to stress is the fact that effective communication is about a process that ultimately is beneficial to all parties.

Some indicators of a listening, reflective school are as follows:

Does the school seek the views of children? How does it do this?
Is there a well functioning and empowered school council that makes real decisions? How do parents' views get heard?
How easy is it to find people willing to serve on the governing body?
How active is your relationship with support services e.g. Police, Fire Brigade, Nurses, Doctors? etc.
Are local churches and faith groups involved?

Thought for the day

Kind words can be short and easy to speak, but their echoes are endless.

*Mother Teresa. (Agnes Gonxha BoJaxhlu)
1910-1997. Albanian Roman Catholic nun who founded the Missionaries
of Charity in Calcutta in 1950, working with the poor and destitute.*

Respect for Everyone and Everything

Thought for the day

Respect for ourselves guides our morals; respect for others guides our manners.

Laurence Sterne.
Born November 1713 – Died March 1768. An Irish-born
English novelist and an Anglican clergyman.

Gathering a group of teachers together and asking them why they joined the teaching profession can be an interesting and thought provoking exercise. The answers might range from, 'wanting to make a difference', through, 'I am passionate about children', to, 'someone inspired me'.

Taking a group of children and asking them the same sort of question: 'Why do you come to school?' The answers maybe illuminating but not always complimentary about schooling: 'Because I have to!; I've got no choice!; To get a good job!'

It is unlikely, 'because I enjoy it,' or, 'because I feel valued' is high on the agenda!! Yet when children feel respected in school, school becomes a more enjoyable place to be.

The following is often stated about a school yet very rarely defined: **'There is something special about that school – you feel it when you enter'.** I believe it has much to do with respect and enjoyment, not just from the children but the whole of the school community. And that ethos quickly embraces everyone – an infectious presence that rejects no one.

When I was a 'wet behind the ears probationary teacher' I was fortunate, although I didn't recognise it at the time, to work with a head teacher called Mr Maddison. He made it very clear to me that my philosophy of education would underpin everything that I did. Philosophy, what philosophy!? He quickly put me straight on that matter. "Sampson, your philosophy is as follows:

'As a teacher who has chosen to work in my school you will respect all the children in your class and as a professional you will do everything possible to earn the respect of the children in your class'.

I didn't realise at the time the profound effect those words would have on the following forty years of my teaching career. Throughout my career I have tried to stay true to that philosophy 'imposed' upon me all those years ago. Interestingly a philosophy not just taught as words but demonstrated in practice by, to me, a giant of education. For Mr. Maddison not only was able to talk the talk, but walk the walk.

Nothing seemed too much trouble for him. He appeared to be in the right place at the right time. He diffused issues before they got out of hand and encouraged and enthused at every opportunity. Mr. Maddison not only respected children, he also respected all those connected with his school!

Though you may not choose the same philosophy, for yourself, I do believe it is important to have a personal philosophy or set of guidelines that will influence and create a firm foundation for the way you work in schools.

Robust Discipline Policy

Thought for the day

It is one thing to praise discipline, and another to submit to it.

Miguel de Cervantes.
Born September 1547 – Died April 1616.
A Spanish novelist, poet, painter and playwright.

A dictionary definition of 'Robust' is as follows: Robust means healthy, strong, durable, and often adaptable, innovative, flexible.

A good discipline policy should not just be about behaviour but a way of life, both in and out of school. The policy must be known by all involved with the school community and its success is measured by the way people adhere to it.

The positive qualities of a discipline policy must not go unnoticed and will be apparent by those who administer it and those who are its recipients.

A robust discipline policy needs to be:

1) **Healthy:** *A fit and healthy body doesn't happen by accident. The body benefits from exercise, eating a balanced diet and being generally aware of the positive effects a healthy body will bring. The same can be said for the discipline policy.*

The exercise is in its regular use.

The balanced diet is about how it is used and received.

The benefits are the positive outcomes for the individual and the school.

2) **Strong:** *Its strength is based upon the fact that it must underpin everything that goes on within the school. When discipline is given high priority all other things will fall naturally into place. Good discipline will embrace teaching and learning, creating a safe environment for the whole school community.*

3) **Durable:** *A durable friendship can be defined as a lasting and stable relationship. It is helpful to look upon an effective discipline policy as a good and valuable friend. It lasts because its value can be seen and experienced. And its stability is based upon the fact that it creates a stable community in which to be.*

4) **Adaptable:** *Just as school is an organic community so must the scaffolding be that is used to support its growth. The policy needs to change with the times, creating greater sense of peace, purpose and prosperity. If the policy remains on the shelf its life will be limited. Its mode of operation should be active and energetic and able to move with the times, informed by regular, rigorous monitoring and evaluation.*

5) Innovative: *Not just one dimensional but able to be shaped to meet the needs of the people who are the school community. The policy must be successful in its outworking and, when it is, it will spawn new ideas as well as further developments. It won't stand still. The changes will build on the positive outcomes created by its productive use.*

6) Flexible: *Prepared to change to accommodate the needs of the school it serves. It is vital the Behaviour Improvement Plan is the servant and not the master. By that I mean it must serve the community and not dominate the way people work. The plan must be open to modification and ready to change as its use is evaluated. To quote the well know credit card advert: 'It must be looked upon as our flexible friend'.*

There are times when the completion of a policy document brings a sigh of relief to authors and readers alike – Phew, it is finished! But a discipline policy can never be looked upon as finished for it should be a living tool, breathing new life and growth into the society it works amongst.

Treat it as a respected ally and it will serve you well.

Section Two

Behaviour Improvement – Planning to Practice

Thought for the day **When putting something in its proper place it not only has to fit it has to be effective.**

The Three R's: Rules, Rewards and Repercussions

Thought for the day

In schools there can be too much emphasis on the management of behaviour rather than the coaching and modelling of positive and acceptable behaviour.

As carers and workers with children we are not, in general terms, responsible for the behaviour of the children in our care BUT we are responsible for managing their behaviour.

And hand-in-hand with this must go the coaching of positive and acceptable behaviour. In any Behaviour Improvement Plan the following three essential elements – all of equal importance - must be in place. I've termed this 'The Three R's'.

R one: **The Rules.** The code of conduct.

R two: **The Rewards** associated with following the rules.

R three: **The Repercussions** of choosing to not follow the rules.

These **Three R's** act as the framework for the Behaviour Improvement Plan. Rules, along with the rewards and repercussions are part of the process that helps to coach good behaviour. In Section Two we will be looking in more detail at the Three R's and how a school might arrive at and implement them. But where and how do we start?

Introducing the Behaviour Improvement Plan:

To enable good behaviour management to take place there must be a behaviour improvement plan that is known and used effectively by all stakeholders, connected with the school. The aim is to ensure that the managing and coaching of children's behaviour is consistent in all aspects of the life of the school.

The plan must involve the whole school community and be effectively communicated. Fundamental to the implementation of the **behaviour improvement plan** is that its focus must be a **'Process for praise and not a procedure for punishment'.** It must create a safe, as well as a warm environment for the children to work in. In addition it must enlist the support of the parents.

How do we ensure that everyone is rowing the school boat in the same direction? The headteacher, as coxswain, is crucial and needs to steer the boat in the right direction. S(he) must make sure that the sails are unfurled and are catching the wind of change. Because of their position in the boat the head can see all participants.

The headteacher needs to take control and lead through the following process:

1) *Outline the aims of the whole programme.*

2) *Decide upon the process initially rather than the detail.*

3) *Involve everyone throughout the process, so that it is 'owned' by all.*

4) *Ensure that everyone is involved as equals.*

5) *Recognise that some teachers are further along the road than others – i.e. the behaviour of the children in their care is good.*

When change is to be implemented in a school, steps need to be put into place to make the change as smooth as possible.

The seven steps for change.

A - Ask: Prioritise communication. Acknowledge the staff's skills and experiences. Staff need to be consulted to express concerns and opinions.

B - Benefits described. Highlight the benefits and how it will enhance their work.

C - Create a shared vision. – Shared across all stakeholders so people feel part of the bigger picture.

D - Digest in bite size chunks. Break the process down. Change requires a 'Work in Progress' attitude. Tackle change in stages. Look at the outcomes that need to be achieved.

E - Engage the children. Include the ideas of children.

F - Foundations. Plan ahead. Build solid foundations.

G - Get practical. Look at the issues and come up with common sense solutions. Keep it practical.

Ideas to support the Behaviour Improvement Plan:

- **Make it real and involve everyone.**
- **Complete the audit identifying good as well as suspect practice.**
- **Identify and quantify the issues regarding attendance/ lateness/ other key issues.**
- **Report the concerns to the whole staff and the governing body.**
- **Arrange consultation with parents and children.**
- **Put into place a set of actions that can be seen by all as addressing the issues and concerns highlighted.**

If it is recognised that something needs to be done about the behaviour of the children in the school then steps need to be taken. However, what sort of steps might the school need to take in establishing an effective behaviour programme that will make a difference? Below is a model that schools could follow regarding such a process:

A circle for change

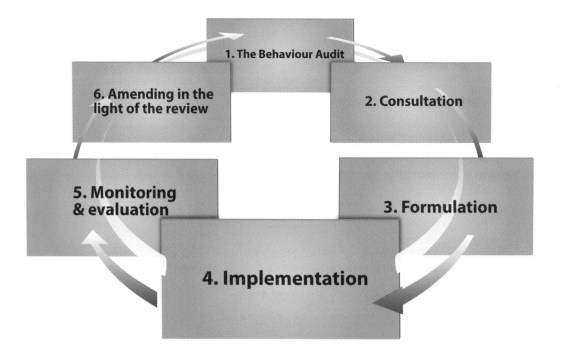

The Behaviour Audit

Thought for the day

To look is to open your eyes. To identify is to see. To respond is to have vision.

The behaviour audit is the starting point. Reviewing practice, procedure and performance in schools has now become a way of life. Although subjective evaluation is important, dotting the 'i's' and crossing the 't's' through an objective process enables schools to use the evidence obtained to support and inform future development.

Simply Behave encourages the use of a 'behaviour audit' that by design can be tailor-made to suit the requirements of any school. To do this well requires an investment of time and effort - but more work today means much higher levels of satisfaction tomorrow for the whole school community. The information gleaned from this easy-to-use process will help you to evaluate your present discipline procedures as well as influence any changes you might consider making.

If there is a concern about behaviour in the school it can act as a trigger for the use of a behaviour audit with the audit providing a litmus test as well as informing future development.

The audit process is carried out in five clearly defined stages, which can be done in any order.

(i) *Asking the children.*

(ii) *Conducting a bird's eye view of the school.*

(iii) *Discussing with staff.*

(iv) *Involving the governors.*

(v) *Consulting the parents.*

The sum of the above will provide different perspectives on the issues and should be looked at holistically to give you a rounded picture.

(i) The Behaviour Audit - Asking the Children

Thought for the day

Asking children their views will enable you to have a better view of them.

It is essential the children are involved, not only in the review process, but also in developing any changes emerging from their involvement. It is important to take the views of a cross section of pupils to including both genders, a range of ages, abilities, ethnicity, disabilities, as well as attitudes to school.

You can involve as many children as you like but as a rule of thumb the minimum number required should equate to 2 children for each class in the school.

For example 7 classes = 14 children.

As already stated the make up of the group is vital, representing a cross section of the school population:

a) *Age.*

b) *Gender.*

c) *Ability.*

d) *Ethnicity.*

e) *Disabilities.*

f) *The good and the not so good as far as behaviour is concerned.*

When asking the children their views on the '3 R's' (Rules, Rewards and Repercussions) it is better to interview the children one at a time, enabling the children to voice their own opinions without being influenced by the responses of others. The answers can be recorded on a grid, with the Key Stage Two matrix differing from the Key Stage One matrix in the sort of language used.

Key Stage 1 Matrix

Name of child Which class are they in?	Are the rules you use in your classroom put on the wall? Any others?	Can you tell me please a rule you have in your classroom?	If you behave nicely in your class what does your teacher say or do?	If someone is naughty in your class what might your teacher say or do?	Do you behave nicely in class?	What sort of nice things do children say to you?	Has any child in your class tried to help you this week? How?	What do you like best about your class?	Is there anything else you would like to tell me about your class?

Key Stage 2 Matrix

Name of child. Which class are they in?	Are the rules of the class displayed in your classroom?	What are the rules of the class?	If you follow the rules what sort of rewards do you get?	If you don't follow the rules what sort of things can happen to you?	What do you think of your own behaviour?	What is good about the behaviour in your class?	If you wanted to make the behaviour even better what would you like to see happen?	What is not so good about the behaviour in your class?	Anything else you would like to say about behaviour?

This questionnaire is very much class focused and will strongly reflect the children's views on behaviour as it affects them in the classroom. It is my experience however that the classroom is a mirror for school. If, however, you feel you would like to explore the children's views of the school simply replace the word 'class' by 'school'.

Once you have collected the data from the selected children you will begin to see several pictures emerging.

e.g.   *What life can be like for children in their classrooms.*

   How individual children view the classroom and each other.

   Whether the rules are clearly established and effectively applied.

   There will be confirmation of some of your views.

   There might be some surprises emerging from the exercise.

Whatever the results it is important to use the data given by the children to move things forward.

Feedback to the children should always be provided after a consultation with them has taken place. This will enable them to see what impact their involvement has made in the outcome of the wider consultation exercise.

(ii) The Behaviour Audit - Bird's eye view of the school

The next step in the behaviour audit is what I've termed the 'Bird's eye view of the school'. This means a designated member of staff has responsibility for going round the school, filling in the chart that follows and making appropriate notes. This is best done when the school is empty of children e.g. before or after school starts and finishes. This only needs to be carried out once and can be done very quickly. Of course, a school may decide to ask the class teachers to complete the grid as another way of doing this part of the audit.

Venue	Rules displayed	Rewards displayed	Repercussions of not following the rules displayed	Class wide evidence for support of the rules	Mission Statement on view
Library	X	X	X		
Dining Hall					
Classroom 1					

Column One: Venue

This first column refers to areas of the school where children meet in groups for work, recreation, study or meeting with designated members of staff. Relevant venues for Column One would be: classrooms, offices, dining hall, assembly hall, gymnasium, library, drama studio, music room, computer suite, withdrawal rooms, parents' room, conference facilities, medical room, toilets, T.V. room, staff room, art room, corridors. Any other space utilised for the teaching of children or adults.

Column Two: Rules Displayed

This second column refers to the rules themselves. If the rules are to have any significance in the school they should be displayed clearly in all areas where users of the school meet. This acts as a constant reminder that:

a) the rules are important and

b) they need to be learnt and followed and

c) they apply everywhere.

The rules should be clearly displayed in a language appropriate to the users of the venue. They should also reflect the rules agreed by the school.

(Advice to the Auditor: It is helpful to make a note of how many rules are displayed, where they are displayed and ease of access/viewing of the rules for the users of the room.)

Column Three: Rewards Displayed

This third column refers to the display of the 'Rewards for following the rules'. These Rewards should be clearly displayed in a language appropriate to the users of the venue. The Rewards should reflect the Rewards agreed by the school.

(Advice to the Auditor: It is valuable to make a note of the way the Rewards are displayed e.g. 'In accordance with school policy' is sufficient. Equally important is where the rewards are displayed – In close proximity to the Rules is key.)

Column Four: Repercussions of not following the rules.

This fourth column refers to the display of 'Repercussions' if children don't follow the rules. They should be given as much prominence as the rules and rewards.

(Advice to the Auditor: Again you should note where and how these repercussions are displayed.) It is important that the repercussions contain a **severe clause**. (This is a clear indication of what sort of behaviour is totally unacceptable e.g. physical violence towards a teacher.)

Column Five: Evidence of class wide reward systems

Information about class wide rewards can be found *on page 172*. Can you find evidence that these are being used in each class of the school e.g. marbles in a jar, or pebbles in a pot or bean bags in a bin – with targets clearly displayed as well as progress towards achieving the targets?

Column Six: Mission Statement.

The mission statement is about the whole ethos and philosophy of the school. Much of what is recorded on the mission statement must be supported by all school policies and in particular the behaviour policy. It can be very simple and is often most memorable when it is simple, for example:

> # Simply Behave Primary School is a community where good behaviour and learning go hand in hand.

(iii) The Behaviour Audit - Discussing with staff

If you monitor staff room discussion, high on the agenda would be the behaviour of children in the school. From comments like 'How have Year X been today?' to 'Y was up to his tricks today'. For many teachers the success of any lesson is gauged by the way the children behave. i.e. Well behaved children = Well taught lesson. Interestingly, though, Badly behaved children = Badly behaved children, and not badly taught lesson!

What is very important for any school is that underlying issues such as poor behaviour must not remain underlying. There needs to be every opportunity for teaching staff to be able to discuss behaviour in a constructive, objective and non emotional way.

Reminders that the behaviour of children is not normally the teachers' responsibility but the management of it is will remove the propensity to accuse or excuse a 'struggling' teacher. The aim is to diffuse the situation and to focus on the strategies they can use to bring about a resolution to the apparent revolution going on in the classroom.

All staff/phase/year group meetings where curriculum is being discussed should also have **a five minute slot on behaviour.** To ensure this doesn't take over the whole meeting the following advice should be considered:

- Where does the slot go in the meeting? Beginning is probably best.

- What form should it take? Discussion followed by an action.

- How can we ensure it is only five minutes? Guillotine discussion after five minutes – with a reassurance to individuals that there will be an opportunity to discuss it further after the meeting. (Please note if the issue becomes bigger than expected it is important to create time at an additional meeting to discuss the issues raised).

(iv) The Behaviour Audit - Involving the Governors

The governors should always be involved in all stages of the change process, kept informed of all the plans and consulted with as "critical friends". As well as the normal reporting on behaviour e.g. exclusions and suspensions, which focus on the bad news, it is also very important to report on the rewards handed out to children e.g. 12 good news letters home, 16 Bronze, No loss of golden time, Attendance award won by Year 6 with 98% etc. Not only will this help the governors to receive a balanced picture of the school, it will give the headteacher a more focussed and realistic evaluation of behaviour issues within the school.

(v) The Behaviour Audit - Consulting the Parents

You may decide that consulting the parents, will be done at a later stage, helping to evaluate any changes the school might make in the light of information gathered from (i) – (v) above. Whenever it takes place the **why**, the **what**, the **when** and the **way** of this consultation process is very important.

Why consult with parents? We value the contribution of parents and that is why we are asking for parents' opinions! There is much wisdom in the statement united we stand divided we fall. When parents are asked about any issues, particularly behaviour, it can cause on the one hand unnecessary anxiety – 'Is it really that bad in the school?' - or at the other extreme 'About time something was done, expelling is too good for some of them!'

To enable the school to get the very best from the children it needs the support of the parents and carers. Without their willingness to support the school in positive ways school will always remain in a 'them and us' position. I've experienced the damaging effect on children when parents openly encourage dissent on the part of their child, with demands such as: "If that school says anything about that earring you are wearing you come home and tell me and I'll sort …..etc".

Consultation is about listening to the views of others as a way of helping to inform the way forward. To make it worthwhile it needs to be more than just a paper exercise, so that all those who contribute feel that not only have they been valued but their views and opinions have been taken on board and acted upon. Although this process can be time consuming it will certainly prove to be helpful and beneficial. Feedback to the parents should always be provided after a consultation with them has taken place.

What do we want to consult about?

The past, the present and the future.

As outlined already this can be done in the form of a simple questionnaire. What the school is trying to establish is:

a) *What the parents think of the discipline in the school.*

b) *How it might be improved.*

c) *The role they can have in that process.*

d) *The way they can support the school.*

e) *The way they can help in the monitoring and the review of the whole behaviour improvement plan.*

When should we involve the parents?

Once the decision has been made to consult, the next step is when that consultation process takes place. At what stage in the timescale of formulating the behaviour improvement plan are the parents' views sought?

It isn't easy to state categorically when and how often this should take place, as it will vary from school to school. A suggested guideline might be as follows:

- Enough times to create confidence.

- Not too often to create anxiety.

- Not too little to create uncertainty.

- As part of evaluation, review and monitoring.

The way to consult with parents: The school can choose between a variety of ways e.g. letter, open meeting, questionnaire, home visits. A letter is a good way of preparing the way. The following are suggested models for a covering letter and possible questionnaire, listing some of the questions a school might like to consider asking parents and carers.

Dear **Friends of the school,**

We are always looking to improve what we do at our school. As part of the ongoing review process we will be looking at the behaviour improvement plan that we have in place at the present time.

Although we are very happy with the behaviour of the children in the school we want to make it even better. We want to ensure that over the next three months all of you have an opportunity to have a say in the development of the new behaviour policy.

There will be four stages in the process:

1. A questionnaire about discipline in the school for you to fill in with your child if you wish to.

2. A meeting to discuss the results of the questionnaires and to establish the way forward.

3. The details of the new behaviour improvement plan and how the school can work with you to implement it for the benefit of all.

4. A review process based upon the monitoring system put in place to check the effectiveness of the new programme.

With this letter is attached a questionnaire that we would like you to fill in to enable us to gather information to help the way forward.

Yours etc.

Questionnaire

1. What do you think of the behaviour of the children in school?

    Very good   **Above average**   **Below average**   **Poor**

2. How does your child view the behaviour of the children in his/her class?

3. Do you know any of the school rules that are associated with behaviour? If so what are they?

4. Does your child know any of the school rules associated with behaviour? If so what are they?

5. When your child behaves well what sort of rewards might s(he) get?

6. What reward has your child had recently for good behaviour?

7. If a child doesn't behave well what sort of repercussions (punishments) might they receive?

8. What sort of repercussions (punishments) has your child seen a teacher use during this week?

9. Do you think it would help if the school rules were written out for you so they could also be used at home?

10. How do you think school and parents can work together to make the behaviour in school even better?

11. Any other comments you would like to make.

Please note the responses to this questionnaire will be made known to all parents who make a contribution. But please be assured, no names will be divulged.

Rules

Thought for the day

If you want the children to toe the line then the line has to be clearly drawn.

Most of you reading this book, would class yourselves as law abiding citizens. However, I wonder how many of us find that we have broken the rules. Just imagine for a moment sitting behind the wheel of the car. Picture the scene. A relatively clear motorway, a powerful car out for an enjoyable drive. Very soon some of us might find we are travelling at 75mph instead of 70 mph. We are breaking the law: The question is, why?

There are numerous answers from: 'I didn't realise' to 'So are others'. Let us look at some of the possible answers in more detail and see how some can relate to breaking the rules in the classroom.

Motorway: Scenario Speeding. Excuses.	Classroom: Scenario – Not following the rules. Reasons.
I didn't realise.	I didn't know that was a rule.
I was in a hurry.	My own agenda takes priority over the rule.
Everyone else is.	I wasn't the only one.
Silly rule 70mph.	I think the rule is stupid.
My car is built for going faster.	I'm known for my misbehaviour.
The road is perfect for going fast.	The classroom lends itself to bad behaviour.
The chances of being caught are almost nil.	Teacher can't do anything about it.
Can't see the point.	Couldn't care.
I get a thrill from speeding.	It is great fun when we misbehave and I get attention.

Although many of the reasons for speeding might be well known to us we also would be honest enough to admit that if we spy a police car, and we think we are speeding, the impact on the footbrake is immediate – in fact the motorway can suddenly become a mass of red brake lights. Why? Because we don't want to get caught. We don't want to suffer the repercussions.

The teacher, to take the analogy further, is 'The Police Car' of the classroom. However, there are teachers who don't have the effect of reducing the incidents of bad behaviour in their classrooms. This can be for a variety of reasons e.g. lack of experience, circumstances, status, presence etc. However, I know, whatever the circumstances, behaviour in the classroom will be improved when the teacher not only has effective resources at their disposal but is also equipped to use them.

In relation to rules, the first thing I feel it is important to stress is that **the rules should be agreed by the whole teaching staff** and by that I include all other staff involved in the everyday teaching of the children. This is certainly a new way of thinking, for in the past the importance has been stressed of pupils having a real voice in the formation of the rules. It is my assertion that the pupils must have a say, **not** in the rules **but** in the instructions – this is explained later on in the chapter.

Imagine you are sitting comfortably in the seat of your holiday plane, looking forward to a well deserved holiday. Suddenly the pilot of the plane approaches you and, after explaining it is his very first flight after training, asks you for a couple of rules to help fly the plane! Panic or pleasure, confidence or confusion, sitting or sliding!? Exactly, you as a passenger would expect the pilot to be in full control and know the ropes. I firmly believe that as teachers we should be in full control and set the rules for the school. We may not be in control of a plane but I would suggest our 'passengers' are equally precious.

What are the key principles for defining the behaviour rules?

1. The rules must be about behaviour.

2. They must be observable.

3. They must be for all times i.e. 24/7.

4. They must be for all circumstances and in all situations.

5. They are different from instructions.

6. They can be used by parents/carers at home, when the children are away from school.

7. There needs to be as few as possible. A maximum of three.

Keeping in mind the 7 principles listed, there are three rules that, it can be argued, cover all eventualities. The rules are not listed in any order and are only written as guidelines for schools.

The Three Diamond Rules:
(After all they should last forever!)

Rule number One: Follow instructions with thought and care.

Rule number Two: Show good manners at all times.

Rule number Three: Care for everyone and everything.

Or in appropriate language for the younger children in the school:

The Three Diamond Rules:
(for Lower Key Stage One)

Rule number One: Please do as you are told.

Rule number Two: Please be polite.

Rule number Three: Please be caring.

Rule Number One: Follow Instructions with Thought and Care.

On the surface this sounds a straight forward rule with little room for misunderstanding contained within the six words. However, if not taught and used properly it can create a mine field of difficulties for the users. Above it was stated that <u>rules</u> numbered **three**. During the day children will receive, and teachers will give, **many** <u>instructions</u>.

Instructions are time-limited and tend to be specific to a particular activity e.g. To bring an end to break times the teacher on duty blows the whistle and the children stand still. The blowing of the whistle not only signifies the end of play it is also an instruction for the children to stand still.

OR. When listening to a story and the children are sitting on the carpet the instruction might be 'don't lean on anyone or anything'.

The two important distinctions between rules and instructions highlighted by the two examples above are as follows:

1) The children can help to define the instructions: e.g. When reading a story what instructions shall we have today children?

*   'Make sure you can see the teachers face at all times'.

*   'Don't lean on anything or anyone'.

*   'If you can't see the pictures at given times please raise your hand.'

These instructions can be decided upon by the children BUT when the story is finished these instructions need no longer apply.

2)   If a child chooses to lean on the bookcase or on another child the RULE the child is breaking is **'Follow instructions with thought and care'** – so you don't get unhelpful or apparent nit-picking conversations like: 'John received a warning today because he leant on Jenny'. Instead: 'John received a warning today because he chose not to follow a given instruction' – clearly breaking the school rule of: 'Follow instructions with thought and care'.

This clear distinction between **rule** and **instruction** avoids confusion as well as abuse of the rules. Once this idea is clearly established it is easier for all people involved.

It is key before that start of any lesson or activity that the children know the particular rule and have a say in the instruction to be followed. e.g. A Science lesson may start by the teacher emphasising a rule: **Care for everyone and everything.**

Additionally the teacher may decide, depending on the age of the children, to elicit, from them, an instruction: **Instruction** (arrived at by the pupils): **Don't touch anything on your table unless permission is given by an adult in the room.**

All members involved in the lesson now know the parameters in which the lesson is to be conducted.

To help the children arrive at an appropriate instruction there can be a 'bank' of them displayed in the classroom.

Of course there are many other instructions that would be necessary for the children to follow when in the care of adults in and around school. Whatever instructions the children have to follow there should be a clear distinction between rules and instructions.

Thought needs to be given to school trips as well as travelling on public and private transport. Once again the school rules will remain but the instruction will change according to the differing circumstances.

There now follows some examples of Instructions a school might use.

You will notice that they all contain the word 'please'. There is a school of thought that using the word 'please' is somehow inappropriate when giving out rules and instructions. The use of please is not pleading but a firm yet polite way of talking to the children. In addition the children will be encouraged to use the same phraseology when giving other instructions to their peers: For example: 'Please pass the book Anil'.

Examples of instructions a school might use

In the Classroom

Please put your hand up to ask a question.
Please use the appropriate classroom voice.
Please make sure you can see the teacher's face at all times when they are reading a story.
Please don't lean on anything or anyone.
Please don't touch anything on the table/desk unless the teacher gives permission.
Please listen carefully when you are being spoken to.
Please move around the classroom in a sensible way.
Please don't make a sound with your mouth when leaving the classroom.
Please line up with a thought for others in the line.
Please sit in a sensible way.

Outside – in the school grounds

Please stand still when the whistle goes.
Please play in the designated areas.
Please act in a responsible way with given equipment.
Please make sure your games are safe and sensible.

Outside the classroom but within the confines of the school building

Please move around the school in the most efficient and sensible way.
Please be sensible in all areas of the school.
Please wait sensibly if waiting is necessary.
Please help others when help is required.
Please walk into the hall without making a sound with your mouth.
Please don't do anything that would set a bad example to others.

Rule Number Two: Show Good Manners at All Times.

One of the hardest jobs for children today is to learn good manners, especially if there aren't good examples set by others. The two key aspects of this rule are <u>to show good manners</u> and <u>at all times.</u>

The underlying principle is that the children need to be taught good manners and have ample opportunities to use them without fear of ridicule. In addition they must be shown them by both their peers and adults within the school.

There is an endless stream of good manners that children will embrace as well as come to terms with. Although the following list is not exhaustive it will help as an aide memoir for all users:

Audio: These are the words you would hear when good manners are employed:
Please…..Thank you……Using given names………Excuse me.
I'm sorry…… May I?........Kind words etc
It is helpful to have a growing list on the classroom wall.

Visual: These are ways of visually showing others the use of good manners:
Open doors, hold doors open, pass things politely, smile appropriately, eye contact, thumbs up, allow someone to go before you.

Kinaesthetic: These are the things you can practically do when demonstrating good manners:
Shake hands, Hold hands, friendly pat, a hug, a reassuring touch, help someone up etc.

Demonstrating of good manners is something that needs to be practised, praised, promoted and taught not just by adults in the school but by the children as well. You may find the R time programme a useful resource, here, as it is based upon the belief that good manners are an essential ingredient in the formation of positive, respectful relationships and that that good manners will result in improved behaviour. *(See information about R time on page 167)*

The overt use of good manners can be considered as being 'over the top' but I believe it is better to have an 'over the top' approach to good manners than no approach at all. Yes a balance is required and this quickly materialises once the initial 'honeymoon' period has passed.

Showing good manners is not an intellectual exercise and neither is it about memory. Good manners are a way of life and, once they become an automatic response, the community in which we work and live will become a far more caring place to be. To promote good manners is to embrace care, not just for one another but for everything as well.

Rule Number Three: Care for Everyone and Everything.

Thought for the day

Consider

All

Respect

Everything

Without a sense of caring there can be no sense of togetherness. The school is a community that extends far beyond the school grounds. For community is all about people and the number of people who have an interest in a school is immense.

Each school must not only foster care but enable everyone involved with the school to add to the caring ethos. To give people a chance to care is vital but of equal importance is to appreciate and recognise that care e.g.

- Does the school council have on their agenda issues regarding the fabric of the buildings? – Playground markings, colour of toilets, placement of curtains, table cloths in the dining hall, etc.

- During whole school assemblies are there awards that specifically highlight someone's care for a part of the building?

- In the classroom does care for the room go unnoticed or is it rewarded and valued by the other members of the class?

These kinds of approaches create not only opportunities for caring but also empower those who take seriously the responsibility of caring for the building. The buildings, whether new, old or in between, must be looked after to enable the school to fulfil its purpose. The ethos of the school will be reflected in the way the bricks, mortar and grounds are cared for – and this is not the sole responsibility of the care-taker but of all members of the school community. It is very easy to make the leap from the well tended buildings to well tended children. The opposite is equally true – uncared for school, uncaring occupants!

But care for the community goes far beyond buildings and must address the vital issue of caring for people. Treating them with respect, not because of what they do and say, but because respect and care is woven into the whole fabric of this living and growing community.

Just as opportunities are created to reward and recognise care for the buildings, so must care for the people who use the school facilities be rewarded. But underpinning those rewards must be the fact that caring for others is a reward in itself. Care starts from within and manifests itself in the way we treat others. Caring attitudes and natures will create a sense of well being and purpose. A sense of safety and security. A sense of one-ness and family.

Implementing the rules

Once the rules have been agreed there are other key elements to consider before the rules will start to have an impact on the school.

1. The rules need to be taught to all school users.

School, by definition, is a close knit community. Most people will be there for 40+ hours each week. Although not a place for uniformity it should be a place for unity. A place where everyone should be working for the good of everyone else. The best way of creating unity is to establish common goals and agreed ways of achieving them. To enable others to play a valuable part, and not feel a spare one, is to establish goals that all can achieve and therefore succeed at.

Rules can be taught and reinforced in many ways.

For example – Assemblies through the reinforcement and promotion of the rules by those leading the assembly.

PSHCE opportunities that specifically deal with the school rules. This can be done once every half term demonstrating the importance of rules as well as the need to learn them.

Class time when the children have the time and space to revisit the rules in a familiar environment through activities like R time and Circle time.

The Primary and Secondary National Strategies on Behaviour and Attendance offer schools practical materials to help develop social, emotional and behavioural skills. It is most helpful if schools familiarise themselves with the SEAL curriculum.

2. The rules need to be modelled as part of the learning process.

The diamond rules: Follow instructions with thought and care;

Show good manners at all times;

Care for everyone and everything;

could be argued, are a good framework for working with, not just children, but others as well. The power and the impact of these rules is not just about the telling of them but the showing of them. Telling demonstrates knowledge; showing demonstrates commitment and belief in them. Demonstrating good manners is contagious and is key in not just setting a good example, but in teaching respect and courtesy. Children quickly grasp the value of displaying good manners by the way they are praised and received by their peers and the adults around them.

3. They need to be displayed as attractively as possible in all areas of the school where children gather.

The small print on a document or legally binding contract can often catch us out and so can rules badly displayed. It is important that the rules are attractive in the way they are presented and I have seen some beautifully produced Rules' Posters. They need to be able to be seen from a distance and able to be understood by the readers. When the rules are well known and well used the actual posters serve as a constant reminder that the rules are to be followed and valued as a principal part of school life.

An inspector, when visiting a school said, to a group of 6 and 7 year olds, "Well, you all seem to know the school rules, but I don't see any lists on the walls?"

A 6 year old girl replied, "Miss M. says, that if it is in our heads and our hearts, we do not need to put them up on the walls".

Sadly, not all schools have a saint for a head, or cherubs for children – and all schools have people who need informing and reminding.

4. They need to be written in the language appropriate for the children concerned.

Although the rules within the classroom stay the same, the way in which they are written and displayed can change to suit the age and needs of the children. Simplifying the words is not easy but there will be occasions when it is necessary e.g.

Follow instructions with thought and care could be written, *'Please do as you are told.'*

Show good manners could be written, *'Please be polite'.*

Care for everyone and everything could be written, *'Please be caring'.*

5. They need to be communicated effectively to all other stakeholders in the school.

This has far reaching implications for everyone involved in the school, for this isn't just about letting others know, it is involving them in the use and application. Educators believe, quite rightly, that children should not be islands in the learning sea; they must have the help and support of others. Managing behaviour in school is about setting standards of behaviour in, around and out of school and it is equally important that everyone sings from a very familiar song sheet. Dual standards of behaviour can only serve to confuse and minimise the effect that well considered school rules help to achieve. The majority of the stakeholders will come on board when they come to terms with the simplicity of Simply Behave. By keeping it simple you will keep it effective.

6. They need to underpin the whole life of the school.

To behave or not to behave is **not** the question. There must be an **expectation** that everyone <u>will</u> conform to the agreed rules of the school. The best way of ensuring this will happen is the positive involvement by the educators as well as the children. A well conceived and thought out moral code will quickly establish a way of living that creates harmony and acceptance.

Rules have a powerful influence on our thoughts, feelings and behaviour as well as our relationships.

Rules, written and unwritten, are defined and reinforced by the way the society in which we live uses and supports them.

For rules to be effective they need to be associated with rewards and when necessary with repercussions. In my experience schools tend to major on the repercussions or sanctions or consequences to the detriment of the rewards.

Rewards

Behaviour management should always be viewed as a **Process for praise** and not a **Procedure for punishment.**

The Elton Report noted that a rewards to repercussions ratio of at <u>least</u> 5:1 is an indication of a school with an effective rewards and repercussions system.

One of the most important things a teacher can do is motivate children, and the giving of rewards is an excellent motivating strategy. The rewards themselves have a far greater value than their intrinsic worth. They will, when used appropriately:

- Establish goals for personal achievement: 'When I listen I will learn'.

- Motivate as well as encourage children to give of their best: 'It is great to be rewarded for effort as well as attainment'.

- Help to ensure that effective teaching and learning takes place. 'It really is a pleasure to learn and teach in such a positive atmosphere'.

- Underline and value qualities as well as activities that are worth pursuing. 'I am beginning to understand what is required to be an effective member of the community'.

- Raise the self esteem of children and make them feel valued. 'I value the recognition that keeping to the rules brings about'.

- Create opportunities for all children to succeed. 'I like it when I behave well for I am rewarded'.

- Take a positive message outside into the community. 'My award reinforces the fact that I am doing my best in school'.

The following must be considered when looking at rewards for good behaviour:

1. The need for **consistency** among those who have the responsibility of administering the rewards.

2. **The way that the reward is 'presented' is important** and signals its value (not just administered in a matter of fact way, but awarded with some degree of praise and admiration. Also acknowledging the rule or instruction that the recipient of the reward has followed).

3. **Make sure that the praise given is genuine** and not just a matter of routine. If you have to look hard to find good behaviour then the harder it becomes to give a genuine reward.

4. **Keep the whole process of rewards exciting, fresh and vibrant.** This will not only excite pupils but those who are responsible for administering the reward system.

5. **The rewards for good behaviour should be directly related to the rules and instructions** agreed within the school.

6. **Make sure the rewards do not signal that schooling is not valued** - e.g. having the day off, permission to miss a certain lesson, arriving late on a certain day, being excused homework for a period of time are not appropriate rewards and may undermine the value of schooling.

7. **Make sure the rewards are** just that and **not bribes.**
    NOTE: Bribes are given in anticipation of behaviour, for example, "If you listen to the story without talking you will receive a sticker."
    Rewards are given as a result of good behaviour. For example, "Thank you for listening so well to the story. Please come and get a sticker."

7. **The rewards should be displayed** alongside the written rules and be given equal prominence. If the rules are written colourfully on A3 paper then the rewards should be displayed in the same way.

8. **Regular monitoring and reviewing** of the system to ensure that the rewards are having a positive effect on school and child behaviour.

The acronym **P.R.A.I.S.E.** is a useful way of **displaying, as well as activating,** the rewards.

P.R.A.I.S.E.

Parents informed

Rewards given

Awards presented

Intuitive awards that match the child

Specials, specially chosen

Encouragement of good behaviour

P – Parents informed (Phone - call, letter home, word of mouth, an invitation to meet the class teacher or giver of the reward – be specific).

When good behaviour is valued, recognised and acknowledged before others it will create an excellent motivating factor in encouraging good behaviour in the school. However, it is also important that others 'outside' the school community are aware of good behaviour – and it is vital it is communicated to them. This can be done by letter, a phone call, a reward card system that the child is able to take home. The key is the formal establishment of a system that parents and carers know. Praise for good behaviour in school can be reinforced by praise at home. This form of recognising good behaviour has, by definition, a way of prolonging the reward. e.g. the letter home may take a day to arrive and the parent or carer may add to the reward by giving a further reward.

The possible downside to this form of reward is the fact that there is an in built delay to the actual reward as well as the danger that the parent or carer doesn't acknowledge the reward and give it as much significance as the school does. Although both these things can happen this must not be used as an excuse for not giving rewards in this way. In time this situation may change as the message 'hits home'.

R – Rewards (Immediate: sticker, pencil top, rubber etc. – be specific).

It is vital to build into any system for celebrating appropriate behaviour rewards that can be given straight away. There are some key aspects in the giving of rewards:

1. They should be immediate during the day on which the appropriate behaviour was recognised.

2.   The reward should be of value to the recipient of the reward.

3.   The reward should be presented as a thing of worth.

This type of reward is often teacher specific and may depend on the age of the children as well as the sort of rewards the teacher is keen on giving. There can, of course, be a uniformity of gifts within the school and age ranges but I get the sense that there is more excitement and surprise when there is a diverse nature to the giver as well as the gift. Having said that, it is also important to have a school wide reward system that is recognised across the whole school and crosses the ages and gender.

A – Awards.

These are often given at a specific time of day in specific situations. They can be certificates, rosettes, medals, commendations etc. presented daily, weekly, monthly, termly or even yearly.

Awards tend to be the more formal aspect of the rewarding system. They can be given at some formal 'ceremony' that can be class based, phase based or even whole school based. This form of presentation can create the excitement of 'looking forward to'. Once again the awards must be given on the prescribed day or at a prescribed time. If this does not happen it not only devalues the awards but the children receiving them.

The appearance of the awards is as important as the reasons for giving the awards. Scruffy bits of paper, scribbled down names, or outdated awards will not have the desired effect. It is important to remember to present the award in the special way it deserves.

The actual awards themselves can fall into three categories:

    a) *Objects*
    b) *Visits*
    c) *Opportunities*

Object awards:

I will not attempt to list all of them, there are far too many. Their value lies in the fact that they have been earned for some recognised act, attitude or service. Some of the more obvious are as follows:

•   Certificates – often designated bronze, silver, gold and platinum. Once you have gained the bronze the next target is silver and so on.

•   Headteacher awards - a form of a certificate with space to write the reason for the award.

•   An award given by the school council. The school council itself considers who should receive this prestigious award from names given by other children. This award can be given weekly or is on the agenda for every school council meeting.

- Medals that are awarded for a special contribution to the well being of the school. These are highly valued and therefore hard to achieve and rarely given. Associated with them can be an additional treat or reward.

- Some of the more unusual ones might be:

a) *Small gifts that are exchanged for earned tickets for example a key ring for five good behaviour awards.*

b) *An item of school uniform.*

c) *A piece of equipment that can be used in school: for example a fountain pen, a special printed pen or pencil. A ball or skipping rope.*

d) *A tabard that can be worn for a specified period of time, a reminder to all the children about the wearer's special achievement.*

e) *Objects donated by outside agencies or speakers, for example a Bible from the local vicar. A book from the librarian. A first aid book from a nurse.*

Visit awards:

Although these will have an educational value they also need to be seen as a treat. They will act as an award for an outstanding contribution to the life of the school. These are given usually as an end of year or term award and can bring together children of all ages. In addition to children, perhaps the parents can be invited, making a real family occasion. Naturally the cost for the children is subsidised or paid by the school. Visits can include local places of interest. Ten pin bowling establishments. A boat trip. A coach ride. A trip to a theme park or an adventure place. Stately homes that may have animals as a major attraction. These can be limitless and will be seen as an enormous incentive for children and staff alike.

Opportunity awards:

The creative mind can have a field day with the sorts of awards on offer here. They can create in the children a sense of excitement. These opportunities can be class, phase, key stage or school based and will certainly reflect the age and particular opportunities the school can bring to the situation. The list of opportunities should be known by all the children but the excitement lies in not knowing which might be available at any particular time.

It is important to stress here that the opportunities should not devalue school or school work – for example the following are not acceptable rewards: arriving 15 minutes late for school, missing homework for a week, going home early on a given day, not wearing school uniform (if uniform is the norm).

A list of some of the more popular opportunities follows. This might help to explain the excitement this type of award can bring, providing, as it does, opportunities to children and staff alike.

A list of opportunities

- Sitting on a special, decorated table at lunch time with a selected friend. (N.B. It is important on these occasions to give the child an opportunity to bring a friend so that the child is not isolated from his or her peers. It will also ensure that the opportunity is seen as an award and not a 'punishment'.)

- Watching a video during the lunch time break with a friend.

- Sitting in a recognised place of privilege during assembly. (Once again the choosing of a friend or classmate is important).

- Being selected to represent the school at an important gathering or a prestigious event.

- Showing a visitor or new child/parent around the school.

- Being allowed to ring a bell or buzzer to indicate a time during the day.

- Having special supervised access to a computer during the break times.

- Being given the first choice of after school club options.

- Calling the register at a given time.

- Distributing fruit, milk or biscuits if and when appropriate.

- Being the first in the line after or before breaks.

- Doing their work in a specially selected place or area.

- Choosing the songs for assembly and having that recognised.

- Bringing in appropriate music to play as the children come into or out of assembly.

- Having first choice on play equipment or apparatus at break times.

- Having the choice of not having to queue at lunch times.

- Being chosen to take on an extra responsibility, for example, answering the telephone.

- Having your name placed on the honours board.

- Being invited to have refreshments with a senior member of staff.

I - Intuitive Rewards.

There is no doubt that the receiving of rewards will nearly always be a positive incentive. However, there are times when the reward can be a disincentive and can create anxiety for the child receiving the 'so called' reward. There will be times when you need to consider matching the reward to the child in question. I have called this the intuitive reward.

On the second day into my Headship I remember hearing a seven year old boy read. After the experience I gave the boy concerned an 'I am a good reader' sticker. I asked the child where he would like the sticker. His response was immediate. He lifted his jumper up and said, "On me tee shirt". I thanked him for his quick response and then questioned him further about why he apparently wanted the sticker hidden from the view of others. Again the response was brief and to the point, "I don't want my mates to know I've been reading to you!"

I was mildly amused but also shocked and saddened by his response. Here was my attempt to value what the child had done in a tangible way, yet to the boy concerned this was not an honour but a potential source of embarrassment. It also enabled me to begin to understand the sort of culture some of the children were experiencing in the school – where academic success could result in teasing from peers. This was a culture that needed changing.

This incident made me stop and think about the reward system in general. When a child receives some sort of positive recognition it has to be in the form of an acceptable (to the recipient) reward and not a potential banana skin. As a staff we began to consider the rewards given, not just in terms of the reasons, but also in relation to the individual children. Two things quickly emerged:

1.   The vast majority of the rewards were indeed appropriate for all children.

2.   There needed to be a change in the culture of the school that, in certain quarters, 'being good' was almost outlawed.

To enable us as a school to come to terms with this reward issue the answer was relatively straightforward, i.e. Ask the child if they were happy to get the reward and whether they were equally pleased that their friends would know about it. Once this routine was put in place the challenges of matching the reward to the child, and therefore creating a real reward, was greatly improved.

However, it is important to point out here, there was also a real desire on my part as headteacher to ensure that the concerns expressed by the boy earlier would not be duplicated in other areas and potentially create a culture of mediocrity in the school. It was essential that good reading, and therefore children who read well, were not only recognised but universally applauded. But that is another story!

S – Specials.

Some areas of responsibility can be given in recognition of good behaviour. These are given as a short tem special responsibility for children to contribute an area of service to their peers, teacher, class or school, as a way of showing they can act responsibly. Specials give children the opportunity to contribute not only to their own well being but the well being of others. Special Services would be the generic term but 'Jobs', 'responsibilities', 'monitor', 'prefect' would also fit the bill.

There are certain principles to be considered when awarding specials:

1. They should be identified as additional responsibilities to the normal and efficient running of the class e.g. tidy the classroom should be the responsibility of all the children and not a small group.

2. They should be promoted in a way that makes them feel special. Cleaning the sink is a debatable privilege for many children!

3. They should be changed on a regular basis, at least once every half term.

4. The sort of Specials you use can be as creative as you like.

5. If a child is not able to carry out the responsibility well then that 'Special' should be taken away from them – but when the Specials are changed they become part of the team again.

6. With the majority of Specials the children can work in pairs. In fact with some of the Specials it is essential, for example, carrying the lunch box, crate or basket.

As well as the anticipated kind of duties such as delivering the register, there are some Specials that may be of the more quirky type. The following are meant to be examples and not some that might be right for you to adopt. I have used all of these and have found them especially useful for developing relationships with the more challenging children, who may be reluctant to relate to teachers in general and authority in particular. This approach helped me run an efficient and well behaved class even in the most challenging of circumstances. (If you are reading this book and you had one of these jobs, with me, please remember you were the exception to the rule!).

> i)   Shirt monitor. *(Informing me if my shirt was hanging out).*
>
> ii) Tie monitor. *(Informing me if my tie wasn't straight).*
>
> iii) Bristol Rovers monitor. *(Informing me how my favourite football team got on, the day after they played).*
>
> iv) Shoe monitor. *(Informing me if my shoes were dirty).*
>
> v)   'Is my desk tidy?' monitor. *(Informing me if my desk is tidy).*
>
> vi) 'Where is my brief case?' monitor. *(I lose things!)*

A list of suggested 'Specials' follows:

*   Sharpening pencils.

*   Giving out or collecting in books.

*   Light monitor (responsible for the switching on or off of lights in the classroom).

- Lunch Box monitor.

- Answering the class phone on behalf of the class.

- Taking the register.

- Taking messages around the school.

- Money monitor.

- Taking the dinner register.

- Milk and or fruit distributor.

- Operating the classroom blinds or curtains.

- Putting on the classroom music when or if required.

- Keeping the class wide rewards systems up to date.

- Holding the classroom door open if and when required.

- Changing the classroom calendar.

- Being the classroom librarian.

- Watering and looking after the classroom plants.

- Giving out whole class equipment.

- Collecting in whole class equipment and storing it properly.

- Giving out letters to the class.

* Please note.. Some of the responsibilities are such that they can give children authority over other children: for example, 'collecting in the books'. Some children initially may give cause for concern if they are given such a responsibility as they may abuse it and cause hurt to other children. Think carefully about matching a 'Special' to a particular child.

E – Encouragement

Although this is the last to be addressed, it is certainly not the least important. In fact it underpins all other forms of rewards. We need to be constant encouragers to the people we work with and care for. 95% of our day should be the way of the encourager. This is not about empty 'well dones' and 'that was fantastic', when it isn't. It is about encouraging others in specific and meaningful ways. There is a wonderful, anecdotal story told about Michelangelo. He was asked what he was carving when he was observed chipping away at a huge untouched block of marble. His response, **"I am releasing the angel from within."**

As people who work with children part of our task is to release the angel from within.

This is a two step process:
a) *Seeing the angel within,*
   and
b) *Having the resources and abilities to reveal it.*

One of the greatest resources we have at our disposal is encouragement. This isn't just about throwing encouraging words haphazardly into the arena, or even directly at and to children. It is about encouraging children **to think, to listen, to follow instructions, to relate well to others, to give of their best, to ask questions, to focus on given tasks, to concentrate** for appropriate periods of time and so on.

To encourage is not an optional extra, it is a vital tool of our profession. When involved in teacher observation I used to put a tick every time I saw or heard a teacher use encouragement in a positive and constructive way. In addition I placed an asterisk by the tick if the encouragement got the desired effect from the child – I can say with a great deal of certainty, ticks were nearly always accompanied by an asterisk – in fact the teachers used to ask me how many 'T-As' they got (T for ticks and As for asterisks).

Encouragement is a powerful tool. Use it wisely and well – the results can be really impressive.

Class observation that focuses on encouraging children:

This sort of observation should be carried out as part of the teachers' professional development. In my experience teachers, as well as support staff, have found this very focussed approach to lesson observations very helpful indeed.

Having a teacher videoed and wired for sound during an observation can serve as an excellent aid in discussing the whole issue of rewards and their impact on children during lesson time. Although this sounds a very daunting prospect it has proved very beneficial when used in this way. Finding a volunteer teacher isn't always easy!

As someone instructed to carry out the observation the following points should be considered:

- Tick when you hear a positive word of encouragement directed to a child or group of children.

- When the child or children respond positively to the form of encouragement mark the tick with an asterisk.

- Indicate when there are other forms of encouragement used.

- Indicate when reference to a rule or instruction is made.

- How do you feel the children are responding to the 3 R's (rules, rewards and repercussions)?

- Make a note of any repercussions used.

An observation matrix for highlighting the use of encouragements.

Encouragement		Rule/Instruction.	Response from children.	Rewards and repercussions used.	General comments. (To include activity observed as well as date and class or group)
Work	Behaviour				

Column One: 'Encouragement Work … Encouragement Behaviour'
This column provides a simple way of recording every time the children are encouraged by the teacher in the classroom. However it is important to differentiate the reasons for the encouragement 1) For Work.   2) For Behaviour. Of equal importance is recognising the need for a balanced response to encouragement and praise. Please note, however, there are times when encouragement will mainly be for behaviour because of the nature of the activities undertaken by the children, for example, an activity that has a focus on listening tends to lend itself to behaviour focussed encouragement.

Column Two: 'Rule and Instruction'
It is important that the children as well as staff are aware of the behaviour context for the lesson or activity. Before the start of the session the teacher should indicate the rule. The children should have the opportunity to decide on the instruction.
For example: The activity is Numeracy. The Rule highlighted by the teacher is 'Follow instructions with thought and care'.
Instruction decided by the children is 'Use our 30cm voices (very quiet voices, e.g. a voice that travels 30cms).
By establishing the rule and instruction the teacher has established specific parameters within which to praise the children. The children are also aware of the way in which they are to behave.
Please note if a child, for instance, demonstrates good manners it should not be ignored even though it was not highlighted as the key rule.

Column Three: 'Response from the children'
This column is used to record specific responses from individual children, small groups or the whole class. This acts as the barometer for the activity. The column can be as detailed as the needs of the session demand The more challenging aspects of behaviour may need specific mention.

Column Four: 'Rewards and Repercussions used'
It is vital that rules, rewards and repercussions go hand in hand. This isn't to say every time a child follows a rule or an instruction there should be a 'gift' as a reward. Remember 95% of the rewards given should be in the form of praise, encouragement, affirming what the child is doing. It is important to note here that any evidence of the use of class wide rewards should be recorded.

Column Five: 'General Comments'
This is the 'anything else worth recording' column. Apart from the date, class and activity anything of note and help for the teacher and children can be written in this column.

Activating the reward scheme:

Just as the rules are displayed prominently in all areas where children meet for work or recreation, so should the rewards be. The rewards should have the same prominence as the rules and should be as well known. The following pointers must be considered when looking at the whole issue of how to reward children for following the rules:

1.   Display the rewards in an appropriate form and an appropriate way.

2.   Teach the rewards. This will help the children to learn them.

3.   Make sure a letter is sent home to parents to explain the new approach to rewards.

4.   Referring to the rewards frequently is an additional way of learning them as well as giving them value and importance.

5.   Make sure you use them and not abuse them. Remember they are rewards and not bribes.

6.   The rewards should not be used in a competitive way, particularly between children.

7.   Consider, how do you record the rewards and to what purpose?

8.   Check the frequency of usage of the different types of rewards within your classroom.

      A) Encouragement.   B) Rewards.   C) Awards.   D) Specials.   E) Intuitive.   F) Letters home.

Thought for the day
Children are our hope for the future. <u>And</u> we are the hope for theirs.

There is an ABC of behaviour rewards, providing a host of ideas to start you thinking at *Appendix 6, on pages 170-180.*

101 Ways To Praise A Child

(Amended – original author unknown)

Wow. Wonderful. You're special. Outstanding. Excellent. Great. Good.
Neat. Well done. Remarkable . I knew you could do it. I'm proud of you.
Super Star. Nice work. Looking good. You're on top of it.
You're catching on. Now you've got it. How clever. Good job. That's incredible.
Brilliant. Remarkable job. You're Amazing. You're a winner.
You make me happy. Hip, Hip, Hooray. You're important. Magnificent.
Beautiful. Fantastic. You're on target. You're on your way. How nice.
You're Spectacular. You're Unbelievable. Super. Super Job. Beautiful work.
Good for you. Nothing can stop you now. Dynamite. You're fantastic.
Awesome. You're Top Class. Fantastic job. You've discovered the secret.
Bingo. Great discovery. You're a real trooper. Marvellous. Terrific.
You're really with it. Outstanding performance. You tried hard.
You figured it out . What a good listener. You're a treasure . You're great.
You're top notch . That's correct. You tickle my heart. What an imagination.
You learned it right. You're incredible. Now you're flying. Bravo.
Beautiful. I like what you are doing. I respect you. You're sensational. Phenomenal.
A+ job. Hooray for you. You're unique. You care. Creative job. You belong.
You brighten my day. Super work. That's the best. You made my day. I know you are brill!
Beautiful sharing. You deserve the best. You're important. You've got a friend.
You're a joy. You make me laugh. You're A - Okay . You're number one. I trust you.
You are perfect. You're wonderful. A big pat on the back.
Exceptional performance.

P.S. Remember, a smile is worth a thousand words!

Repercussions of not following the Rules

Thought for the day

If you mess up the rules you could end up being a 'luser'.

There will be times, despite the best possible management of your class, when children will choose not to follow the rules of school and classroom. The **'Repercussions'** are there as a means of correcting behaviour that is disruptive within the school. When this 'disruptive' behaviour occurs it must be dealt with calmly, quickly, consistently and in line with the established and well known procedures. Repercussions, along with the rules and rewards are part of the process that helps to coach good behaviour. In schools there can be too much emphasis on the management of behaviour rather than the coaching of positive and acceptable behaviour patterns.

It is essential you are well prepared. By the careful planning of repercussions you will know in advance what to do when children choose to misbehave. You won't be caught off guard or left wondering how to respond to children's misbehaviour. In this way children will be treated fairly and there will be less stress all round. The key to effective repercussions is that they are applied consistently and fairly. Repercussions are actions that children know will occur, should they choose to break the rules. They must be seen as natural outcomes of inappropriate behaviour.

It is important repercussions are presented to children as a response to the decision they made to break the rules. Just as a child makes a conscious effort to follow the rules so there is a decision on the part of a child to break them. When this happens the teacher is placing the responsibility where it should be, <u>on the child.</u>

The repercussions must be clearly displayed alongside the rules and rewards. They must be communicated to all stakeholders in the school. The children must be taught the repercussions and know that parents will be informed if the children continually choose not to follow the rules.

The repercussions are not bribes; they are the automatic result of children choosing inappropriate behaviour. Repercussions must not be used as a threat but as an inevitable response to poor behaviour. They do not have to be severe to be effective. It is the inevitability of the repercussions, not the severity, that makes them effective. The easier it is for you to administer the repercussions the more likely it is that they will be used. It is important that you agree with the repercussions you may be called on to use.

Repercussions must be something children don't like, but they must never be physically or psychologically harmful. Repercussions do not work in isolation. They must be balanced with positive support. The repercussions should be framed in such a way as to reflect a discipline hierarchy. It is important to have a severe clause within the list of repercussions.

The hierarchy is progressive and should start with a warning. The repercussions become gradually more substantial for the **2nd, 3rd, 4th, 5th** and **6th** time that a child chooses to disrupt.

A hierarchy of repercussions

First time a child chooses to break a rule: A Verbal Reminder.

Second time a child chooses to break a rule: Warning that is recorded by an adult.

Third time, a Time Out within the classroom: – 12 minutes maximum (Year 6). 10 minutes for Year 5 and so on. Sand timers are very useful for timing.

Fourth time, a Time Out in another teaching area: – 15 minutes maximum (Year 6)
10 minutes maximum (Year 1).

Fifth time, The child is taken / removed to a designated member of Senior Management Team and Senior Managers and governors are informed, as well as parents.

Sixth time, 'In school suspension:' Minimum of one 'lesson'. Parent sent for.

First Time: Verbal Reminder.

The **verbal reminder** should be just that, and phrased accordingly, with the use of the child's name concerned as well as highlighting the rule not followed. The purpose of this reminder is exactly that, to help the child focus on the correct behaviour as well as pointing out the fact that the incorrect choice of behaviour has come to the notice of the adult in authority. The verbal reminder is related to breaking one of the following three rules. The root is the rule that is being broken:

•   Show good manners at all times: for example – being rude.

•   Care for everyone and everything: for example - using a pencil in an inappropriate way.

•   Follow instructions with thought and care: for example – isn't sitting sensibly,
         constituting a possible danger to self or a nuisance to others.

Four steps to follow when giving a child a verbal reminder as a way of signalling inappropriate behaviour:

1.   Use the child's name.

2.   Indicate to the child the rule being broken.

3.   State the effect that breaking the rule is having, or potentially could have.

4.   Say what will happen if the child persists with the wrong sort of behaviour.

For example: "John I'm reminding you that you are *not showing good manners* when you call out in class. It is also setting a bad example to others. Please stop doing it because if you continue I will have to give you a recorded warning. Thank you."

"Casey, I've asked you to sit quietly when I'm telling the story. Moving around in that way is _not following my instruction_. It is also disturbing others. Please don't let me have to give you a recorded warning for making the wrong choice regarding your behaviour. Thank you".

The whole tone of your voice should be one of genuine disappointment allied to the real desire of not having to discipline the same child again. It also helps to serve as a reminder to others of the rule and instruction.

Second Time: Recorded Warning.

Once again the rule that the child chooses not to follow will be one of the three rules known throughout the whole school. **The recorded warning** must be the natural progression for any child who chooses to break a rule for the second time during a given period of time. (No longer than a day).

The recorded warning is exactly what it says. An adult in the class records the child's name in a designated way, and place. It could be on the board, in a book, on a flip chart, on a display board etc - any way known by the children and appropriate to the age of the class.

It is very important that the child concerned knows they have received a recorded warning and what the next step in the process will be if they continue to misbehave. From experience I find it helpful to read out what is recorded, as it brings a sense of calm and inevitability to the process.

When you initially tell the child about this recorded warning it should have the same four step approach as the verbal warning:

1.   The name of the child.

2.   The rule broken.

3.   The effect that breaking the rule could have.

4.   What will happen if the child continues to make the wrong choices.

The recorded warning should also indicate the specific nature of the misdemeanour:

For example: _"Gurpreet, I have written the recorded warning. It says, "Gurpreet was rude again and was not showing good manners when he shouted across the room, disrupting the lesson. The next step will be an in-class Time Out"._

"Lesley, I have written the recorded warning. It says, "Lesley didn't follow an instruction again when she continued to play with her water bottle on the desk. This disrupted her own learning. The next step will be an in-class Time Out".

The following format may be helpful:

Recorded Warning

Date: 7th April
Name of child: Marie Smith
Rule broken: Not showing good manners – by shouting out
Effect: Disrupting others
Next step: In class Time Out

Once again the tone of the voice should be one of calmness as well as sadness that the child continues to exhibit poor behaviour. The whole reason for this hierarchy of repercussions is because there is a desire on everyone's part to help the child improve their behaviour. It is not about the inevitability of a downward spiral but an opportunity to help the child address some of their issues about bad behaviour.

Third Time: A Time Out in the Classroom:

Just as day is followed by night so a **'Time out in the classroom'** should follow a 'Recorded Warning', if the child continues to break the rules.

A 'Time Out' place in the classroom should be a space reserved for a child, to sit away from other children to enable them to become detached from the normal activities of the day. In its simplest form a Time Out is time without attention. This Time Out place should serve as a visual reminder to all the children in the class that, just as they are rewarded for good behaviour, there will be repercussions for choosing to use bad behaviour. The area concerned should be marked in a way that shows it is clearly a place for thought and reflection. It will almost certainly be a chair with a small desk or table. There should be a piece of paper on the desk where the child's name is to be recorded as well as a timer to indicate the start and end of the time out period. I have also found it helpful if there is some sort of opportunity for the child to sit and use their time constructively in this area. This could be contemplating a phrase or sentence *(Examples can be found in Appendix 7, on page 181)*, the use of a stress ball, or looking at a calming picture. Anything that might help to focus on the right sort of response to the issues that resulted in the chid being placed in the Time Out space.

The length of time the child spends in the Time Out place is important in the sense that it is clearly defined. It is not just about removing the child from the situation that may have helped to create the bad behaviour but an opportunity to calm down and come to terms with themselves. I would suggest that the Time Out should be measured by the use of an egg timer. They can be purchased based upon the times they measure. As a rule of thumb I would suggest 12 minutes to be the maximum time a child should spend in the Time Out space and 5 minutes as a minimum. The timing should not be based on the nature of the bad behaviour but on the age of the child. Therefore a Year 6 child should spend more time in the Time Out space than a younger child.

It is important that the child has a degree of control over the Time Out and should start the egg timer as well as indicate to the teacher when the time is up. When the child returns to their place of working there should be a positive comment from the teacher as a way of welcoming the child 'back' into the main body of the class. For Time Out is more effective when there is plenty of 'Time In'.

The name of the child should be recorded in a book along with the date, the time, the name of the teacher as well as the rule the child chose to break. There should also be a comment regarding the way the child conducted themselves in the Time Out place.

Fourth Time: A Time Out in Another Teaching Area.

Now things are becoming more serious for the child concerned. If a child gets to this stage in the list of repercussions it means the child has chosen to be disobedient four times in a given period of time. (No longer than one day). Despite all that has gone before the child refuses to accept the rules laid down, continuing to make life difficult for self as well as others.

There are seven things that need to be considered when the child reaches this fourth stage:

1. Where will the child go for this Time Out?

2. How long will the child stay in the Time Out room?

3. What will the child do in the Time Out area?

4. Is this the point in the repercussion hierarchy when the child's parent is informed?

5. Is the Headteacher informed about the child experiencing this Time Out?

6. How should the child be received by the 'receiving' teacher?

7. The child will almost certainly need some additional support in helping to improve their behaviour.

1. **Where will the child go?** The key in this part of the process is that the child should go to another supervised teaching area – almost certainly another classroom. The child should be trusted to go unescorted unless:

• The child has previously not arrived at the destination or

• The child is too young to navigate the corridors to the new classroom.

In the unlikely circumstances that the child needs an escort then it must be done by another member of staff and not a nominated child. It is just not appropriate to ask a child to take part in the 'punishment process' by acting as a 'minder' unless it is a much older child escorting a much younger child.

The placement for the child needs also to be carefully considered. I would strongly recommend the following:

a) *The receiving classroom should not be of the same year group as the child being sent.*

b) *There should be a reciprocal approach to the procedure: if you send to class A then you should receive a child from there when a child in that class misbehaves.*

c) *There should be a minimum of a two year age gap: for example 3 to 5 ; 5 to 3.*

d) *You should never send more than two children at a time. *Please note in the exceptional circumstance of four children requiring a Stage Four Time Out send them in two groups of two or even four groups of one using staggered times.*

e) *The room the children go to shouldn't be too far away from their own classroom, if that is possible.*

f) *On the displayed list of repercussions the receiving class should be named.*

g) *If at all possible there should be a separate Time Out place from the Time Out place used by the internal class Time Out process.*

h) *The child should take with them a Time Out slip explaining the reason for the Time Out and signed by the class teacher.*

i) *The Time Out slip will be collected by the receiving teacher and used as a record for the Time Out.*

2. **How long should the child stay?** I would strongly recommend the following:

a) *The Time Out should be longer than the length of the 'in class' Time Out.*

b) *The child should monitor their own time by using an appropriate timer.*

c) *The Time Out starts from when the child has taken their place in the Time Out seat.*

3. **What should the child do during this Time Out?** I would strongly recommend the following:

a) *Something that will occupy the child.*

b) *It could be to duplicate what happens during their class Time Out.*

c) *The child, if possible, should record their name in the appropriate book.*

4. **Are the child's parents informed?** I would urge you to consider the following:

a) *For the first time in the series of repercussions the child has lost their entitlement of being involved in a lesson.*

b) For the first time the knowledge of the child's repercussions has moved out of the confines of their classroom into a wider domain.

c) The only difference between Stage 3 and 4, if parents aren't informed, is the length and location of the Time Out.

d) The reporting of the Time Out to a parent or carer is probably a greater deterrent than the Time Out itself.

e) How will the parents / carers respond to the knowledge that their child has received a Time Out in another classroom?

f) How are the parents to be informed and when?

Please note at some time during the repercussions the child's parents need to be informed, The when and how is a matter for the school to decide – see page 85 for more details.

5.   Is the Headteacher informed? Yes. (And the child must know that).

6.   How should the child be received by the 'receiving' teacher? It is essential that the child does not disrupt the class when they arrive; this is all about how they are received and how the teacher is prepared for the reception.

The reception:

a) Ascertain why the child has been sent, it could be nothing at all to do with repercussions of breaking rules.

b) Quietly yet firmly place the child at the appropriate Time Out place.

c) Explain to the child what they have to do.

d) Indicate to the child to start the timer.

e) Record the child's presence by taking from the child their Time Out slip.

f) It is better to show disappointment than anger.

The preparation:

a) Have your Time Out place ready – table, chair(s) timer and appropriate activity.

b) When the child arrives deal with the situation as soon as practical. If you have classroom support use them to facilitate the Time Out smoothly.

c) At the end of the Time Out send the child back to the classroom with their completed Time Out slip.

Time Out Slip.

(Name of child)   completed the Time Out *(appropriate wording).

Signed by ....   **Date:**...........................

Please note if the child concerned does not co-operate during the Time Out then they should be sent to a member of the Senior Management Team and the child's class teacher informed immediately.

7. **Additional support for the child.** There needs to be recognition on the part of the school that a child who persistently breaks the rules needs additional help. When a child finds an academic subject difficult then help is always at hand, particularly in Numeracy and Literacy. This sort of help would come in the form of extra resources as well as additional teaching support. Sadly there are times when a child who misbehaves just receives more punishment and not much help in trying to break the cycle of bad behaviour. The key in helping the child is identifying the root cause and making every effort to help the child, at best, overcome the issues or, at least, come to terms with them. Not an easy task, but certainly not impossible. An empathetic approach from the school, with diagnosis, before prescription, will certainly go a long way in helping to solve some of the issues.

Although there can be many reasons for bad behaviour there are five main reasons a child chooses to misbehave and it is usually a combination of two or more of them.

a) *Bad classroom management including poor application of the three R's – Rules, Rewards and Repercussions.*

b) *School life in general is too much of a challenge for the child often resulting in lateness, poor attendance, truanting and under achieving - particularly in the area of reading.*

c) *A home life that finds it very difficult to support the child in the right way as far as schooling is concerned.*

d) *The child has issues regarding low self esteem often brought about by factors beyond the control of the child e.g. hygiene, home background, bullying etc.*

e) *Medical conditions can and will have an impact on a child's poor behaviour in school – Aspergers, ADHD, ODD, certain autistic conditions, Tourettes and other Special Learning Difficulties and Learning Differences. When a child is diagnosed with these medical conditions a response appropriate to the individual needs of the child is required - one that assesses what the needs of the child are and which considers how best to help everyone concerned to adjust to and remediate the special needs of the child. (There is more information about these special needs linked to behaviour in Appendix 4, on pages 164-167).*

Fifth Time: The Involvement of Senior Management Team (SMT) and the Informing of Governors and Parents.

If the child reaches this stage of the repercussion hierarchy in the time prescribed (not more than one day) then the child is taken to a designated member of the SMT, more often than not the Headteacher. In addition the relevant members of the governing body will also be informed at the first opportunity.

The senior member of staff records the incident: child's name, time, date, name of teacher(s) involved, reason for the referral. The child is also told that their parents/carers will be informed.

The child will remain with the member of the SMT for a specified amount of time indicated by the 'sending teacher' in the form of an accompanying referral slip. For example:

> **Michael Thompson for the fifth time today has chosen not to follow the school rules by 'Not caring…' (throwing a book across the classroom). If possible could you keep him with you until the end of Science at 2.30pm. Thank you. (Name of teacher).**

It is important to recognise that if a child is constantly reaching this 5th stage of the discipline process (on average once a week) more of the same is not going to have the desired effect.

When a child reaches this stage in the repercussion hierarchy it is highly likely that a variety of other measures will have been put in place: for example star charts, an individual behaviour programme, anything that is tailor made to try and support the child in these challenging times. This could include additional in-school assistance with the child's learning as well as a statement with a focus on behavioural needs and support. Considerable effort may be required, and no stone should be left unturned in trying to help the child come to terms with the anti social approach to their behaviour. These steps to support the child should be well documented and their success or otherwise must be known by those adults directly associated with the child as well senior managers of the school including appropriate governors.

Ultimately, by this stage, Time Outs, warnings, letters to parents have not helped in trying to change the child's behaviour for the better. Additional measures are required. This could involve an input from a specialist, for example: Educational Psychologist, Clinical Psychologist, Behaviour Therapist, Paediatrician, Social Worker, Health visitor, School Nurse, Psychiatrist. When these 'external' agencies are involved it should be with the knowledge of the parents or carers. At this point the CAF process would be a useful way of identifying the best kind of support for the child.

CAF which stands for the 'Common Assessment Framework' is a key part of delivering frontline services that are integrated and focused around the needs of children and young people. The CAF is a standardized approach to conducting an assessment of a child's additional needs and deciding how those needs should be met. It can be used by practitioners across children's services.

CAF is intended to provide a clearly defined process for a holistic assessment of a child's needs and strengths, taking account of the role of parents, carers and environmental factors on their development. Practitioners will then be better placed to agree with the child and family, about what support is appropriate. The CAF will also help to improve integrated working by promoting co-ordinated service provision.

Please note all local authority areas in the UK are expected to implement the CAF, along with the lead professional role and information sharing by March 2008.

Part of the procedure on school governor sub committees should be a brief report concerning these children and their support from the school. It is important to come to terms with the fact that some of these children could end up being excluded for a defined period of time and it is vital that when the names of the children appear before the governing body their history is well known This approach enables the governors concerned to make a judgement based upon all the evidence. Although exclusion is a last resort it should be one that the school is not frightened to use.

Sixth Time: The 'In School' Suspension.

This is exactly what it says. As part of the repercussion process a child may have to serve an 'in school' suspension. The duration for this part of the process is for a minimum of one lesson and for a maximum of a morning or afternoon. It will take place in a prescribed room and involve supervision by an adult. The child concerned will sit for the defined period of time and carry out an appropriate, non fun-filled task.

N.B. It must be remembered that if a child reaches this stage of the process it will have happened during the course of one day, so it is very unlikely that this stage will be reached. If it does, it is vital that a review of the child's day takes place and is documented for future evidence in support of the child and the school.

In school suspensions must continue whenever necessary but there is a danger that children might see them as a soft option. To guard against this the following guidelines should be remembered:

It is not a treat. The children must not be used to take on responsibilities that could be considered to be privileges: For example, taking a message around the school.

Special room established. Initially the room must be established for the sole purpose as an internal exclusion room or area. As the 3 R's become very effective the use of a suspension room should become obsolete and then the room can be used for other purposes. The room must be monitored at all times when children are using it for suspension purposes.

Children sent to the room must work in silence, doing academic work as well as being given the opportunity for some supportive work in trying to correct their difficulties in conforming to the school rules. This should not be about dwelling on the past but looking at ways the school and the child can be helped in overcoming the issues faced by all parties. If the child is disruptive in the suspension room then one of three things must happen:

a) *The child's parent is sent for to help support the school in coming to terms with the behaviour of the child.*

b) *The child is sent home provided all the correct procedures are followed.*

c) *The child is removed from the room and placed in another area of the school that will help to prevent the anti social behaviour continuing.*

It is important that when the child is placed in the suspension room it is for a specific, known period of time.

Parents must be notified that the child is having an in school suspension. The school might also consider the parent being present during this time. If this process is to be used then it is important that the parent is involved in helping the school as well as the child.

Guidelines on the use of repercussions

Check that the children know what the repercussions are and recognise the need for having them.

It is important to **keep track of repercussions undertaken by individual children.**

It is important to **start 'afresh' each new day**. Good and bad deeds will almost certainly be recorded but the children don't need to be reminded if the effect is detrimental to their well being.

Special Circumstances

There are two factors that are important to consider when formulating the list of repercussions:

1) *The severe clause and*

2) *Moving the goal posts for certain children.*

1) The severe clause

The hierarchy of repercussions should include a severe clause for dealing immediately with severe behaviour. It is essential that the school has in place a clear definition of what constitutes a severe incident. A severe clause is in place so the school and children know what behaviour will not be tolerated in school and if it does happen the child will move to, at least, Stage Four in the school's set of repercussions, probably even further. I list the following as incidents that will constitute the imposition of the severe clause:

a) *Bullying.*

b) *The physical abuse of a child.*

c) *The physical abuse of a teacher.*

d) *Racial abuse of anyone in the school.*

e) *Being in possession of harmful drugs for their own use or for 'selling' to others.*

f) *Carrying a weapon such as a knife.*

The following could also be considered by the school as **severe clause** incidents:

a) *Swearing at a teacher.*

b) *Deliberately breaking or damaging school property.*

c) *Stealing.*

d) *Open defiance in carrying out one of the repercussions, for example refusing to go to the Time Out space.*

e) *Deliberately missing lessons by hiding in an area of the school.*

f) *Doing something that constitutes danger to another child, for example pulling the chair away when they are about to sit down.*

Some other issues that might be considered severe:

a) *Cheating to gain an advantage.*

b) *Telling lies to get others into trouble.*

c) *Bringing matches into school.*

In consultation with the governors severe clause incidents may require putting into operation the need for exclusion – whether temporary or permanent.

2) Moving the goal posts for certain children:

This is perhaps a controversial issue, but one the school needs to be aware of and consider. There are children who, because of the nature of the repercussion programme, can view it as a charter to misbehave. For example, they are happy to have a Time Out in another class, it gives them a break. They know the system and know how far they can go before their parents will be informed, so they misbehave up to that point.

The children concerned exhibit this pattern of misbehaviour on a regular basis, so much so, it is almost the norm. Here is clear evidence to suggest that the chid is abusing the system. What is clearly happening here is that the child has taken control of the repercussion process. The question is how to stop it and, by so doing, help the child. The answer can be straight forward.

a) *Demonstrate to the child that you are aware of their pattern of ill conceived, unproductive behaviour.*

b) *Tell the child that you intend to help them to improve their behaviour.*

c) *Tell the child for the period of one week the child will start at Stage Three of the repercussion process. In other words, as soon as the child misbehaves Stage Four will be actioned. The desired effect is incredible – believe me.*

You can move the goal post provided that child knows why and how the post is to be moved e.g. A child that uses the system as a license to misbehave – gets to Stage Three every day and then behaves very well. Eventually start the child on Stage Three!

Please note it is important to stress this is being done to help the child and not as a way of punishing them even more. In my experience it has never been considered unfair by the child because it is done in the right way at the right time.

When to Involve Parents

How do you know when you should contact a parent about an issue? How early in the process? Judgement is needed. Some circumstances are very clear e.g. vicious fighting, racial abuse, a child who refuses to work, extreme violence. In these cases don't think twice about informing the parent. It may be necessary for the school to request the presence of parents in the classroom for those children that are particularly disruptive – this can be a very powerful deterrent.

There are day-to-day instances that are not so clear-cut. Here you must use your experience and your judgement. If uncertain use the 'your own child test'. The test that will put you in the position of the parent:

So – Assume you have a child the same age as the child in question.
      If your child was having the same problem in school would you want to be called?
      If the answer is YES, call the parent. If NO, it is essential that there is an alternative course of action.

Parents **must** be informed towards, or near, the end of the hierarchy of repercussions.

Plan and prepare how to speak to the parent:

1.   Be clear on the statement of concern – and show your concern in a caring way.

2.   Describe the specific problem and when possible present documentation.

3.   Describe what you have done so far.

4.   Enable the parent to have an input into how to solve the issue. Try and listen without interrupting.

5.   Tell the parent what you intend to do to help solve the issue. This should be the main focus of the meeting.

6.   Explain to the parent how they can help. Listen carefully to their response.

7.   Let the parent know you are confident that the issue can be resolved.

8.   Tell the parent there will be a follow-up contact from you.

9.   Recap (briefly) all that has been said.

10.   If possible ensure another member of staff is present during the discussion with the parent.

11.   If the school operates a parent befriender system then by all means agree to the parent having the befriender there.

12.   Remember the context of the meeting. The parent WILL be supportive particularly if there has been previous positive contact regarding the child.

Launching the Behaviour Improvement Plan in your School.

Thought for the day

If you want to launch a big ship then the water needs to be deep!

You have carried out the audit. You have consulted widely and have agreement about the way forward. What next? To launch the new, updated or amended Behaviour Improvement Plan certain factors are absolutely essential to create maximum effect. Clear and decisive leadership is really crucial. It is about making sure everyone in the school is using the new process professionally and productively. This can only be achieved by leading by example, 'Management by Walking About', being around the school, setting an example to the rest of the team. Success in the area of behaviour doesn't always come easily but it will be easier if everyone knows they are supported and encouraged from 'the top'.

In other words taking a lead on:

- this is what we are going to do ..

- this is when we are going to do it …

- this is why we are going to do it …

- this is how we are going to do it ….

- this is how our efforts will be measured….

Procedure to launch:

Preparing to launch takes time and needs to be timetabled into the year ahead. Assemblies and PSHCE lessons can provide opportunities to prepare the children and the whole school community for the introduction of the new systems that will underpin the behaviour improvement plan. It will help immeasurably if:

1) *Behaviour improvement is established as a whole school priority.*

2) *Everything is done openly and inclusively.*

3) *All preparation is carefully considered, responsibility is designated for each part and people are released to get on with their role.*

4) *Dates for meetings and implementation stages are listed as stepping-stones towards launch day.*

- **What we are going to do:**

  Set out a starting point for the new plan, to include information given to all stakeholders, with a statement regarding the philosophy of the behaviour programme.

  Ensure the plan and their roles and responsibilities within it is understood by everyone who has a vested interest in the new behaviour process.

  Establish clearly that the emphasis will be on praise – but if children choose not to follow the rules there will be clear repercussions detailed in the plan.

  Money should be set aside in the budget to ensure proper resourcing of the programme.

  A letter prepared to send out to parents and carers explaining the new system and how they can support the school in the successful implementation.

  It is also important to take into account where the three R's should be displayed and how they should be displayed.

  Classes need to establish the instructions they might use.

- **When we are going to do it:**

  Establish a "looking forward" approach to the new plan, generating some excitement. Preparing the way for its inception, to include stakeholders becoming very familiar with the rules, rewards and repercussions.

  Send out invitations for the launch day. For example invitations to an assembly designed to introduce the programme.

- **Why we are making changes to the existing plan:**

  Establishing a rationale for introducing a new plan, to be included in a letter to all key stakeholders (including parents) about the changes is really important. To include a 'before and after' statement of the way forward.

- **How the school will be using the new plan:**

  Rules, Rewards, Repercussions displayed and communicated with all stakeholders in the school, with careful consideration about the wording.
  Posters made and the rules, rewards and repercussions displayed throughout the school.
  Instructions displayed in classrooms.
  Rewards purchased and in place for use.
  Simple booklet designed and produced, explaining the behaviour programme.

Communicating about the plan with the children

A personalised letter, in age appropriate language explaining the new system, will be sent to each individual child.
The children are taught what the rules are, what they mean and how to follow them.
The children know what the rewards will be and how they can achieve them.
The children know the hierarchy of repercussions and the implications for them if they choose to not follow the rules.
Everyone knows how the process will operate during lunch times.

Communicating about the plan with the staff

The staff of the school need to know how to use the new system in the most effective way – both as individuals and as a team.

Communicating about the plan with the governors

The governors must be aware not just of the system but how the children, teachers and parents are responding to it.
The governors need to become involved in the whole process – not just aware but in possession of a full working knowledge.

Communicating about the plan with the parents

The parents need to be encouraged to support the new plan at home. To help with this the children can take home a booklet to explain the new system. This should contain the following: The rules; The rewards; The repercussions. How the process will operate during lunch times. What the severe clause is and the implications for any child breaking any one of the activators for the severe clause.

Children could take home duplicated posters of the three diamond rules for parents to display in their homes and parents could be encouraged to use the same rules, thereby reinforcing their use.

Parents can establish their own reward system that complements that of the school.
They can have their own set of repercussions that can work alongside the school's.

The school could explore running a behaviour management course for parents, or parents and children, to enable the parents to feel better supported with their own behaviour management concerns.

Hopefully, parents will have been involved in the process of developing the plan *(see pages 48-49)*. Now that the new systems are ready for implementation it is important to let the parents know what has been decided. A sample letter, providing the information in a simple format, which asks the parents to show their willingness to co-operate with the school in the carrying out of the behaviour plan can be found on *page 90.*

How the school will measure the successful implementation of the new plan:

It is crucial to establish clear guidelines on how to measure the success of the plan.

In addition to subjective indicators (for example a feel good factor, greater peace within the school, a more relaxed atmosphere, comments from stakeholders being positive) there needs to be objective indicators as well – for example:

- Number of children receiving rewards.

- Attendance figures improved over a period of time by ?%

- A decline in the reported incidents of bullying.

- Break times and lunch times are better managed with a significant number of children receiving green cards.

- A decline of children receiving red cards of ?% since the inception of the programme.

- The names of children who have made a positive step towards improving their behaviour.

- A return to the behaviour audit showing a marked improvement in all the target areas.

Informing parents about the new plan

Dear Parent,

I am delighted that _____ is in my class. With your encouragement, help and support I will ensure that your child will be part of many exciting and rewarding experiences.

It is very important that your child learns about making the right choices, not just in school but also in every day life. The school has developed a new behaviour improvement plan that will help all of the children to make the right choices about their behaviour enabling them to work, learn and play together in a positive way. Your child deserves to have the best possible experience at school and I know that working together will help that to happen. Below is an outline of the school/classroom behaviour improvement plan starting with the rules we will be using in school.

Rules:

1.   Follow instructions with thought and care.

2.   Show good manners at all times.

3.   Care for everyone and everything.

The wording for the younger children.

1.   Please do as you are told.

2.   Please be polite.

3.   Please be caring.

Rewards:

To encourage children to follow theses rules I will be quick to praise good behaviour. In addition when your child chooses to follow the rules they will be rewarded. There will also be termly reports about your child's behaviour in school.

Repercussions:

However if a child chooses to break a rule the following steps will be taken:

1)   First time a child chooses to break a rule they will receive a spoken and polite warning.
2)   Second time in the same day, a written warning.
3)   Third time: a Time Out in the classroom (No longer than twelve minutes).
4)   Fourth time: a Time Out in another classroom (No longer than fifteen minutes).
       Please note if this happens to your child you will be contacted during that day.
5)   Fifth time: the Headteacher, Governors and Parents will be told that the child has had a fifth repercussion in one day
6)   Sixth time: the child will be sent to a supervision room for a period of at least an hour.

Please read this classroom behaviour improvement plan with your child, then sign and return the form below. If you wish to talk to me further about anything connected with the behaviour improvement plan please don't hesitate to contact me to arrange an appointment. (Please note if the form is not returned within the week we will assume you are in agreement with the proposals).

Best wishes,

---✂

I have read the behaviour improvement plan and have talked about it with my child.

Parent/Carer Signature _____ _____   Date _____

Any comments you wish to make?

To accompany the letter to parents, here is a suggested format for the family friendly version of the Behaviour Improvement Plan:

The Family Version of the
Behaviour Improvement Plan

It is very important that your child learns about making the right choices, not just in school but also in every day life. The school has developed a new behaviour improvement plan that will help all of the children to make the right choices about their behaviour enabling them to work, learn and play together in a positive way.

Below is an outline of the school/classroom behaviour improvement plan starting with the rules we will be using in school. As a school we would like you to consider using the same rules at home.

Rules:

1.	Follow instructions with thought and care.	OR Please do as you are told.
2.	Show good manners at all times.	OR Please be polite.
3.	Care for everyone and everything	OR Please be caring.

Rewards:
To encourage children to follow these rules the school will be quick to praise good behaviour. In addition when your child chooses to follow the rules they will be rewarded.

So the children know and remember how they can be rewarded the school has used the word PRAISE:

Each of the letters stands for a way of rewarding the children.

P = Parents   (The parents or guardians of the children will be informed regularly).

R = Rewards   (The sort of rewards will be stickers, smiles, words of praise etc.).

A = Awards   (These will be awarded on special occasions such as assemblies or other gatherings).

I = Intuitive   (This sort of reward will try and match the reward to the particular needs of the child).

S = Specials   (These rewards are designed to make the child feel special in the responsibility they are given).

E = Encouragement   (We believe it is vital that the children are encouraged in their good behaviour as well as their work).

Repercussions:
However, if a child chooses to break a rule the following steps will be taken:
1)   First time a child chooses to break a rule they will receive a spoken and polite warning.
2)   Second time in the same day, a written warning.
3)   Third time: a Time Out in the classroom (No longer than twelve minutes).
4)   Fourth time: a Time Out in another classroom (No longer than fifteen minutes). Please note if this happens to your child you will be contacted during that day.
5)   Fifth time: the Headteacher, Governors and Parents will be told that the child has had a fifth repercussion in one day.
6)   Sixth time: the child will be sent to a supervision room for a period of at least an hour.

Please read this school behaviour improvement plan with your child. Talk about it together. If you have any questions please don't hesitate to contact the school.

Reviewing the Behaviour Improvement Plan

Much emphasis in a Behaviour Improvement Plan is placed upon the **3 R's:** The **R**ules, **R**ewards and **R**epercussions of not following the rules. It is important to stress that the quality and effectiveness of the Behaviour Improvement Plan must not be just about its structure but in how you **implement and apply** the structure that the school has arrived at.

It cannot be stressed enough that the importance lies in the <u>application</u> of the **rules, rewards** and **repercussions** and not just the knowledge of them.

Simply Behave says that the application has six clearly defined parts:

1)   The **formulation** of the rules, rewards and repercussions.

2)   The **communication** of the rules, rewards and repercussions.

3)   The **teaching** of the rules, rewards and repercussions.

4)   The **modelling** of the rules, rewards and repercussions.

5)   The **use** of the rules, rewards and repercussions.

6)   The **evaluation and monitoring** of the rules, rewards and repercussions.

But don't spend too much time reviewing and looking back. All you are likely to get is a stiff neck! There are times when, because we are not sure about how to move forward, we spend all the time reviewing what we have in place. What is important is to identify what is working well and what needs to be altered or fine tuned to enable further progress to be made.

Move forward. If there is a strong sense things need to move then do something quickly.

It will soon become obvious where the strengths and weaknesses are. It is essential to focus on a) The system and b) How it is being used.

For example 1:   One of the three rules isn't understood by the children.
                A solution: More teaching and modelling required.

For example 2:   The teacher doesn't establish the context for the lesson by underlining a rule
                and identifying with the children an important instruction.
                A solution: A classroom observation that focuses on that aspect of the lesson.

For example 3:   One class, or a group of children within the class, are finding it difficult to come
                to terms with the repercussions being used.
                A solution: An observation of the teacher using the repercussions and rewards
                with those children.

Is there a need to fine tune?

Fine tuning is usually concerned with areas of weakness. Change will be needed if there is a groundswell of opinion that says an aspect of the behaviour plan doesn't appear to work or is too difficult to manage.

For example 4:   It is difficult to keep track of the children being given green cards at lunch time. A solution: The children place their green cards in a box within the classroom so the information can be collated at a more convenient time.

Is there a need for a radical overhaul?

A radical overhaul will be needed if there is no discernable improvement in the overall behaviour of the majority of the children despite fine tuning and change being introduced.

The key aspect here is to check that the plan has been introduced in the correct way, taking into account the advice given in the relevant areas of Simply Behave.

Questions to consider:

Have enough resources been put aside to make sure the new process has every chance of succeeding?

Have the classes got sufficient stickers, certificates, small prizes, timers, marbles (if used for class wide rewards) etc.

Is it necessary to set aside a percentage of the budget that will be used to resource classroom based initiatives?

Staff meetings:

These should always have a brief item on the agenda to discuss the system and not the children.

Changes will need to be made in the light of reasoned discussion and not knee jerk reactions.

There will be teething problems but don't throw out the wisdom teeth for the sake of a few aching molars!

How do we involve all the other stakeholders associated with the school?

A half termly meeting with dining room staff is essential as a way of reviewing the lunch time behaviour plan.

A regular slot on governors' meetings is essential that clearly identifies targets around behaviour and how the school is meeting them.

A letter home to parents is essential explaining how well the programme is going and thanking them for their support.

Classroom observation is crucial in monitoring behaviour in the school.

It is vital to consider a) Who should do the observing?

b) When is the observation done?

c) What is being observed?

Specific observation of teaching staff - Look for the use of the following:

P.R.A.I.S.E. – the reward system. (*See Page 61*)

Repetition of rules – particularly at the start of a lesson.

Establishing instructions when working with the children – using some of the instructions suggested by the children.

Use of positive relationship strategies. (See *page 28*)

T.E.A.C.H. (*See page 20*)

How can teachers and other school based staff evaluate their own practice?

Reviewing your practice – a simple checklist

Adults should EXPECT – not ASSUME. We can assume too much. You know what assume does: **'It can make an 'ass of u and me!!'**

Get the basics right:

Look at your room:

1.   Does it support the rules etc?

2.   Are the rules, rewards and repercussions clearly and carefully displayed in pride of place?

3.   Have you established a Time Out place for your own children and children from another class?

4.   Environment – carpet area. Table placement.

5.   When and where are the trouble spots?

6. Are there trouble times in your room? Is the afternoon more challenging behaviour wise than the morning?

7. How can you manage the classroom more effectively?

8. Trouble spots in the school?

9. Is the seating plan based upon classroom dynamics?

10. Where have you placed yourself?

Look at yourself:

What is your role in the whole process?
Teacher as a role model. Teacher as a Professional. Teacher as a Person. *(See Pages 15-20)*
How can T.E.A.C.H inform your working? *(See Page 20-24)*

1. Teach and model the rules, rewards and repercussions.

Principles of rules: In effect at all times.
                 In all activities and situations.
                 24/7.
                 Observable and only relate to behaviour.
                 As few as possible – recommended three.
                 Known by all stakeholders of the school.

Rewards - supportive feedback.
Rewards: P. R. A.I. S. E.
Class wide rewards. Marbles in jar. Dots on the door.

Repercussions – corrective feedback.
The easier the repercussions are to give the more likely you are to use them.
Use repercussions in the prescribed discipline hierarchy – List them in order in which they will be Imposed for disruptive behaviour <u>within a day</u>.

2. Look for behaviour you want and point it out to the class.

3. Think about your language. The thing you ask for is the thing you get. Speak about the behaviour that you want to see.

4. Feed back to the children.

5. Be aware of the classroom dynamics.

6. Redirect if off task.

7. The disruptive child. What do we do about the child/children who still operate outside the boundaries? *(See pages 79, 82, 101, 102, 106)*

8. The severe clause.

How do we involve the children in the review process?

One way is to revisit the Behaviour Audit in respect of the questionnaire for the children. You may decide to use the same children and compare answers looking for positive steps forward.

Or you can use a different group of children, with their selection based upon the previous criteria. Hopefully you might find it more difficult in identifying children who try to operate outside the behaviour programme!

Key Stage 1 Matrix

Name of child What class are they in?	Are the rules you use in your Classroom put on the wall?	Can you tell me please a rule you have in your classroom? Any more?	If you behave nicely in your class what does your teacher say or do?	If someone is naughty in your class what might your teacher say or do?	Do you behave nicely in class?	What sort of nice things do children say to you?	Has any child in your class tried to help you this week? How?	What do you like best about your class?	Is there anything else you would like to tell me about your class?

Key Stage 2 Matrix

Name of child What class are they in?	Are the rules of the class displayed in your classroom?	What are the rules of the class?	If you follow the rules what sort of rewards do you get?	If you don't follow the rules what sort of things can happen to you?	What do you think of your own behaviour?	What is good about the behaviour in your class?	If you wanted to make the behaviour even better what would you like to see happen?	What is not so good about the behaviour in your class?	Anything else you would like to say about behaviour?

Or is everything fine?

If things appear to be going well **don't forget to congratulate everyone involved with the success of the programme.**

In Summary

School based staff need to be informed and involved in encouraging appropriate behaviour by having -

Clear guidelines for responding to appropriate behaviour.

- Three diamond rules in place and known by all.

- A clear statement that for every instruction given at least 2 pupils should receive feedback and approval.

- A hierarchy of rewards for appropriate behaviour, to include class based rewards.

- The approval rate in terms of giving praise and encouragement for following instructions and rules increases at the start of each new activity or lesson.

School based staff need to be informed and involved in discouraging inappropriate behaviour by having -

Clear guidelines for responding to inappropriate behaviour.

- Set out a hierarchy of repercussions, and the arrangements for applying them consistently and fairly.

- Make clear the boundaries of what is acceptable.

- Promote respect for others and the intolerance of bullying and harassment.

- Promote the importance of self-discipline, proper regard for authority among pupils, and the difference between right and wrong.

- Appropriate use of SEN procedure for behavioural problems.

School based staff need to be informed and involved in monitoring policy and practice throughout by having -

- Designated staff meetings for reviewing procedures and practice.

- Regular reviews of provision for individual children.

- Termly review of policy.

- Regular observations throughout the school, by staff, to monitor staff and individual children.

School based staff need to be informed and involved in conducting evaluation throughout by having -

- Implementation of targets set on management plan.

- Regular evaluation of behaviour and discipline.

- Regular evaluations through observations of verbal feedback to classes and individuals.

Section Three

Specific Measures for Specific Circumstances

Introduction:

If we sweep enough dust and dirt under the carpet we will just get lumps and they won't go away if we do more of the same. Sometimes specific measures are required for specific circumstances or the mole hills can become mountains. In this section of Simply Behave we will look at potential issues that can create difficulties in a school if they are neglected and not managed. Ignoring them is not an option and hopefully the ideas outlined in this section will help to ignite new ideas and create unity of purpose and approach.

Challenging Behaviour

Thought for the day
Those who put their finger on the issue will also need to lend a hand.

There are sometimes children who don't appear to respond to the whole school Behaviour Plan. 90 – 95% of the children in the school choose responsible behaviour.

There are, however, the few who will ignore the rules, may not respond to your corrective actions and can disrupt the entire class. Disruptive behaviour can fall into four categories and it is often helpful to recognise these areas of concern:

1)   Off task behaviour:

This sort of behaviour is characterised by the child who cannot settle quickly and quietly to the work they have been given. Their concentration spans are limited to a few minutes. They are unable to focus for any length of time on tasks given, even when they are age and ability appropriate. The child may take to wandering around the classroom or gazing into space or out of the window. They need constant reminding to keep on task.

2)   Disruptive and annoying behaviour:

This behaviour is characterised by the child wanting to call out or make sounds or inappropriate noises. They seem unable to sit still for any length of time and their fidgeting is accompanied by the apparent desire to disturb others. They seem unable to keep their hands and feet to themselves and seem to take a great deal of pleasure from interfering with other people's possessions – hiding things, defacing them, passing them to other children to tease and annoy. They also try to engage children near them in conversation, although it is usually more of a monologue than a dialogue!

3) **Aggressive behaviour:**

This behaviour is characterised by the child suddenly calling out in an aggressive way for what appears to be the most insignificant reasons. This can be accompanied by pushing or knocking over of resources near them. There will be times the child takes to flicking or throwing things across the classroom with intent to hurt others, or at least distract them. There will be instances of name calling but often done in an open way so others in the class will be certain to hear. Sometimes there will be instances of pushing and punching that could escalate into a fight situation. On occasions the child may storm out of the classroom, accompanied by the slamming of doors and the upsetting of chairs or other equipment.

4) **Anti social behaviour:**

This behaviour is characterised by the child refusing to engage with peers or adults. This is not demonstrated in a subtle way but with body language that can be termed as being defiant and rude. Conversely the child makes inappropriate attempts to engage with their peers or adults. For example pinching, pulling hair, making rude or unhelpful suggestions. To attract the attention of an adult the child may make sounds as if they are hurt or complain constantly of other children 'harming' them. These children find it very difficult to make friends and when they do they will find it almost impossible to maintain the friendship. They can become very jealous of other children coming between them and their new found friend – there is almost a suffocating quality to the relationship. These children may exhibit signs of emotional turbulence, for example, unusual tearfulness or an obvious withdrawal from social situations.

It is true to say that the boundaries of these types of inappropriate behaviour may overlap and children may exhibit more than one of the above. However, in many children who exhibit unacceptable behaviour, one of the four will dominate. Trying to address the underlying issue will almost certainly have an effect on the child coming to terms with the other issues of behaviour.

The sort of behaviours described above will be known to you, and the children concerned will often use the classroom as a place to perform their own antics rather than their work. These children can push your buttons and make you forget about being calm and assertive. They need your unwavering determination to help them behave appropriately. They can go through the discipline stages on a regular basis and their behaviour shows only a temporary improvement. Such children can drain your energy.

What can be done?

Children who present difficult behaviour often have very little or no history of compliance with rules. Children with chaotic home lives may only see appropriate adult behaviour at school. Don't lose your composure and don't give up on them. Instead you must try and bring an individualised approach that falls within the framework of your general classroom behaviour improvement plan.

You must first of all recognise and accept that if you are having difficulties so will other children in the class. Remember, if your classroom Behaviour Improvement Plan doesn't work with some children, it is seldom your fault. And it is not the fault of your Behaviour Improvement Plan. However, you may have to go beyond your general plan and behaviour management techniques to reach out to children who find it difficult to conform to the normal patterns of expected behaviour.

With those children it is crucial that a limit setting structure is balanced with a supportive and caring relationship.

Try and look beyond the behaviour and see the child. If you want to be effective in reaching these children you need to show that you care and value them. Children that display behavioural difficulties will rarely reach out to you – *but they might change their attitude if you reach out to them.* Make it your goal to establish positive relationships with even the most challenging children.

You do need to maintain a professional distance, but keeping your distance doesn't mean you keep your relationship within the academic realm. It means becoming actively interested in the children as people: in their lives, their relationships, their friends and interests. *Some simple suggestions that will enable you to get closer to the children are listed on Page 28.*

Personalised Approach

Adapting your behaviour management techniques to suit the more challenging children

The majority of the children will respond well to a one-to-one meeting. Here are some basic considerations to keep in mind:

1. The child must know that you care and you are meeting them, not to punish, but to help them.

2. Tell the child you are going to try and help – but, "We must work together".

3. Ahead of the meeting prepare well. Make sure you are fully conversant with the child's records, talk to the teacher who had the child previously and may be able to throw some light on the situation.

4. When meeting with the child try and find out why they are behaving the way he/she is. It is vital to clearly identify the sort of behaviour the child exhibits, what triggers it, and how to reduce and ultimately prevent it from happening. For example it could be the child's seating arrangement, friction with other children in the class, the work set may be inappropriate for that child, factors from home may be involved, your relationship with the child may be a problem, or there may be a medical concern.

5. Try and remember that the prescription should fit the diagnosis. Aim to help the child to solve the problem e.g. move them, contact home, give more appropriate work, consider introducing an appropriate relationship programme (R time) to encourage positive relationships within the class. Focus specifically on the behaviour you are unhappy with e.g. calling out in class, running out of the room, throwing things around the room.

6. The child needs to be told that their behaviour prevents others learning, as well as themselves, and that their behaviour stops you from teaching the children in the way you want to.

7. Concentrate on one aspect of the behaviour that you and the child know you are unhappy with and tell them clearly and specifically how you would like them to behave:
    e.g. Calling out – "Put your hand up and I will respond to you in an appropriate way and at the appropriate time".
    e.g. Running out of the room – "You must not do that but instead when you feel like running, you may come and sit on the chair next to me".
    e.g. Throwing things around – "It is dangerous and you could hurt someone. Take the piece of paper on the Time Out table and draw a picture of you throwing at a target."

8.   Come to terms with the fact it is a small steps process and things will very rarely be solved overnight.

9.   The results of the meeting must appear in the child's Individual Education Plan (I.E.P.) or 'Action Programme'.

10.   Review and discuss the actions with valued colleagues as soon as is appropriate.

11.   Consider the use of the CAF process to enable everyone concerned with the child and the child's family to agree how to help them.

Remember:

1)   The child must know the specific behaviour expected of them as well as of you.

2)   It may be necessary to provide corrective actions that are not part of the class's behaviour steps – both rewards and repercussions. The rules however remain the same.

3)   Meaningful positive recognition to be given when the child does behave appropriately.

4)   With young children (Year 3 and below) you need to be very specific on how they should behave – role play can help, or the early intervention of behaviour therapists.

5)   With the older children (Year 4+) it is important, where appropriate, to give them a say in how they choose to behave.

6)   You must use the corrective actions you have decided upon each and every time the child disrupts.

7)   You must reward each and every improvement in behaviour. (Rewards to be agreed with the child).

8)   Succeeding in changing challenging behaviour is often long and arduous. It will take perseverance and patience and will require the help of the whole school.

Keep a detailed record of incidents as well as agreed corrective procedures.

Name and class:
Date time and place of incident:
Brief description of the incident:
Actions taken by the teacher:
Agreed way forward:

Evidence of all actions that have been taken must be carefully documented in case it becomes necessary to consider the child being suspended or excluded from school because of further deterioration in their behaviour.

Who needs to be involved?

The individual behaviour improvement plan, agreed with the child, needs to be shared with all adults involved with the child in school.

Keep the **parents** fully informed – at best in a meeting and at least by letter.
Use the **'your own child'** test.
Plan carefully what you are going to say to the parents.

If all attempts to involve the parents, including visiting them at home, are met by resistance or failure, then extraordinary measures must be taken to help the child as well as the school. These could include the school enlisting the help and involvement of other agencies. At this point the CAF process would be a useful way of identifying the best kind of support for the child.

Taking account of the special needs of individual children

Some pupils with more complex behaviour, emotional and social difficulties may fall under the definition of disabled. The definition of disability includes conduct disorders such as oppositional defiance disorder (ODD), Hyperkinetic disorders such as attention deficit disorder or attention deficit hyperactivity disorder (ADD/ADHD), and Syndromes such as Tourette's and other mental health disorders.

There is a section in Appendix 4, on page 164 to give more insight into the nature of these disabilities.

Such disorders do not need to have been officially diagnosed in order for a pupil to be classified as disabled; the impairment simply needs to exist.

Schools need to focus on the individual needs of pupils with SEN or disabilities and other groups defined as being particularly at risk e.g. minority ethnic and faith groups, travellers, asylum seekers and refugees, children looked after by the Local Authority, sick children, young carers, children from families under stress, and any other pupil at risk of disaffection and exclusion. In such cases schools must make reasonable adjustments in the application of their behaviour policy to disabled pupils and make special educational provision for pupils whose behaviour related learning difficulties call for it to be made.

Schools should plan proactively how the schools disciplinary framework should be applied to each of these pupils and ensure that all those in contact with the pupil know what has been agreed. It is crucial that every vulnerable pupil has a key worker in school who knows them well, has good links with home and can act as a reference point for staff when they are unsure about how to apply the disciplinary framework in the case of a particular child.

Particular reasonable adjustments may need to be made for individual pupils, for example in managing potentially confrontational situations. Schools will need to ensure that everyone in the school community understands that there are circumstances in which some pupils may be treated differently from others and why, building this into the behaviour policy and its wording. Providing appropriate opportunities for staff to have training in avoiding and de-escalating conflict would be a key support in this area.

Behaviour management techniques in relation to children who are unsettled and find it hard to concentrate should take account of the following both in school and at home:

A daily routine is really helpful for the child, e.g. The recording of a daily diary, a five minute 'chat' with a designated school based adult, a specific responsibility within the school or classroom.

Be consistent in the handling and managing of the child.

Be specific in your instructions to the child and make clear and reasonable requests, e.g. Wait your turn before lining up.

Set clear and easily understood boundaries, e.g. When entering the classroom to sit at their designated place.

Remove disturbing or disruptive elements from their daily routine, e.g. Ensure they are sitting next to an appropriate partner.

Plan structured programmes aimed at gradually lengthening the child's concentration span and ability to focus on tasks.

Communicate with the child on a one-to-one basis and avoid addressing other children at the same time.

Use rewards (e.g. stickers, tokens) consistently and frequently to reinforce appropriate behaviour such as listening to adults and concentrating.

Use repercussions (e.g. loss of privileges, being sent to their room) for unacceptable behaviour or 'overstepping' of boundaries.

Discuss the child with their parents or carers and see how you can work together.

Attendance and Lateness

In these areas of behaviour the parents really need to be on board. At Primary stage the children have little chance of arriving at school and being on time, if the parents aren't aware of the importance of attendance and punctuality. Remember the vast majority of Primary children are absent or late because parents think the school will always understand and forgive their reasons. Absence or lateness is out of the control of most primary school children. If a child is continually absent or late **it is usually the parents that need tackling.**

Factors a school must consider regarding the issue of poor or irregular attendance:

1.   A child whose attendance is sporadic or poor will find learning more difficult for obvious reasons.

2.   Children who have a record of poor attendance have fewer friends, and those 'friends' they have tend to be acquaintances.

3.   Poor relationships can promote poor behaviour as well as creating isolates within the classroom. This in itself can create in the child a greater desire to be absent from school.

4.   With good attendance having a high priority in schools, those who don't come up to scratch can be targeted by other children in a negative and unkind way.

5.   Many children don't want the role of being the messenger between school and parents. Any messages regarding adverse attendance or lateness should be sent to the parent by text, email or 'snail mail' and not delivered verbally or by note via the child concerned.

6.   Children who arrive late in school and are 'punished' are at greater risk of becoming at best occasional truants and at worst habitual truants.

7.   Children who are singled out for being absent or late can seek the support of their peers, encouraging them to truant or be late as well – a form of bullying.

8.   Children who are absent or late for school on a regular basis have underlying reasons for this. It is important for the school to recognise this, discover what the reason is and then deal with it – often with the help and support of other agencies. The first agency to be involved is the parent:

Tackling attendance problems:

•   Every child should aim for 100% attendance.

•   Focus on all children, not just the known poor attendees – they can be hard to shift!

•   Parents must phone or contact the school on the first day of their child's absence. If the parent hasn't phoned by lunch time the school phones home! Make sure when a parent phones or the school phones you show consideration, but ask when we can expect the child to return to school.

- Send a congratulatory letter home for every child who achieves a 100% attendance, (authorised absences included) over a term.

- Those children who get a 100% attendance over a term get a small prize. They also have their name placed into the draw for an end of year prize e.g. £40 voucher etc.

- All children who get 100% attendance over the year get a special trip as a group.

- The class with the highest attendance gets a weekly award.

- Children who get 100% attendance over the year receive a prize that could include their family.

- Those children who have clearly made tremendous progress with their attendance are also rewarded.

- Invite guests in to give out the certificates for attendance etc. e.g. police, nurse, governor, officer from the Local Authority - etc.

Factors a school must consider regarding the issue of frequent lateness

1. The majority of children don't want to be late and if they are, they can arrive in a poor state of mind.

2. A child who arrives late in school will certainly be in the minority and therefore can stand out from the rest in a negative way.

Thought for the day

Being on time is not about watching (the clock) **but more about waking and walking.**

Tackling lateness

- Have a member of staff, including the headteacher on certain mornings, to stand at the gate and welcome the children and parents.

- Start the school day promptly and only have a very small window for registration e.g. 9.00 – 9.10am in all classes.

- Close the gates at 9.05am so the parents and children have to get in by 'ringing' the bell.

- Hold a meeting with all new parents and emphasise the importance of coming to school on time. Warn parents a firm line will be taken on lateness. We all want to improve standards.

- Latecomers must report to the office and receive a late slip that they must give to their class teacher.

- The classes with the highest attendance and best punctuality gets a weekly award.

Lateness and attendance charts can be displayed in the classroom. Children can input the information themselves.

A half termly letter should be sent updating the parents on how the attendance and lateness drive is going. This can be personalised to show their own child's average against the school's average attendance.

Letter to the parents:

The school should write an open letter to all parents listing why the parents' help is needed in addressing the issues of attendance and lateness. The letter must state clearly why good attendance and punctuality is very important. It should be a supportive letter and not one of condemnation. The letter should contain information about the school situation as well as national statistics. The letter should outline the steps the school is taking and how the parents can help in addressing this important issue. A possible format follows:

Simply Behave Primary School

Dear friends of the school,

Thank you for your continuing support for the school. It is very encouraging to know that you are working with us to help your child to achieve their best.

As a school we want to improve attendance and make sure that the children arrive on time. At present the monthly attendance at the school is x% and we want to improve it by y%. This will help the school to reach the government target set for our school, and will help to ensure that the children are available for their lessons. Each half term we will write to you to bring you up to date with the attendance figures for that period.

In addition, to help the children arrive in school on time, the classrooms will be open and supervised 10 minutes before school starts. The school gates will be closed at ......*(insert time)* and any child arriving after that time will need to buzz Reception to gain access. This will result in the child receiving a late mark on the register. Three unexplained late marks in a term will result in a formal warning for the parents of that child.

All of these measures have been taken to improve the children's education and to meet the government targets which came into effect in September 2007.

Yours sincerely,

Attendance and lateness: Check list/audit.

Parents/carers should:

- Ensure children attend school regularly.
- Notify school as early as possible on the first day of absence.
- Send a note when the child returns.
- Avoid taking holidays during term time.
- Not keep children away from school for trivial reasons.
- Speak well of the school and support the staff.

Schools should:

- Ensure a senior member of staff is responsible for attendance matters.
- Have an expectation that full-time, punctual attendance will be the norm and all absences will be followed up.
- Use Parents' Evenings, Newsletters and other written forms of communication between home and school to raise the profile of regular attendance.
- Have a declared intention to contact parents of all/targeted children on their first day of absence.
- Make effective use of attendance competitions and award schemes (Class and individual).
- Have a commitment to half termly monitoring of attendance levels.
- Have a practice of reporting to governors on attendance matters.
- Have a willingness on the part of all staff to accept that improving attendance is the responsibility of everyone.
- Have a positive culture/ethos that is based upon a firm foundation of respect and care of self and others.
- Practice positive reinforcement.
- Set targets for improving behaviour and attendance with individual pupils.
- Display weekly attendance figures in the school reception area. This can be done as classes, whole school or both.

The Local Authority should:

- Support the school through the central distribution of leaflets, information material about attendance and lateness.
- Check school registers through the use of OMR (Optical Mark Reader) or similar system.
- Recognise that early intervention is important.
- Have a greater focus on Years 2 and 3; and Years 6 and 7.
- Support specific group work for those children identified as being at risk.
- Make greater use of parental prosecution orders.
- Work more closely with social services.
- Advise schools about research findings and good practice.
- Support the school with a visible presence in whole school attendance assemblies etc.

Bullying

First and foremost, bullying of any description is totally unacceptable and must not be tolerated. Bullying itself is a behavioural issue affecting the lives of thousands of school children, their families and their teachers. Very few schools would claim that bullying doesn't exist in their establishment. Sadly this behaviour can still remain unchallenged until it manifests itself as either impacting on someone we know and care about, or as a problem that has become too serious to ignore and maybe even deal with.

National and international research has shown that bullying knows no boundaries of age, race, gender, abilities, disabilities, religion or socio-economic background. It can take many forms; it can be short term or continue over long periods, even years.

What is bullying and how do we recognise it?
Bullying usually has five common features:

- It is deliberate, hurtful behaviour.

- It is often repeated over a period of time.

- It is difficult for those being bullied to defend themselves.

- It is often difficult for those who bully to learn new social behaviours.

- The person who bullies has power over the victim and exercises it inappropriately.

All forms of bullying can be damaging.
There are four main types of bullying:

- **Physical:** hitting, kicking, taking belongings.

- **Verbal or written:** name calling, insulting, racist remarks, taunting, mocking.

- **Indirect emotional:** spreading nasty stories, excluding from groups, forced joining of groups, making threats

- **E-bullying:** using web pages, emails, text messages and phone cameras.

Three types of bullies have been identified:
(Stephenson and Smith)

- Confident bullies, who are physically strong, enjoy aggression, feel secure and are of average popularity.

- Anxious bullies, who are weak academically, have poor concentration and are less popular and less secure.

- Bully/victims who are bullies in some situations and are victims of bullying in others. These children are usually unpopular.

Additional information that schools might find helpful:

Characteristics of the bully
Anyone can be a bully, however certain risk factors may lead a child to bully:

- Witnesses or experiences violence and/or aggression at home.

- Some emotional or traumatic event has taken place eg, bereavement, marital break up.

- Low self-esteem , inability to form lasting relationships.

- A super-ego (a distorted self esteem and expectation of subservience and compliance from others.)

- Low academic ability, sense of failure in school, poor attitude to work and staff.

- Inability to empathise with others.

Today's bully is not the stereotypical school "oaf" of Victorian novels. They are often difficult to identify because they may be popular with other pupils and have many features that endear him/her to staff. They are often perceived to be articulate, confident, assertive, energetic and even charismatic. They are unlikely to stand out from the crowd, using "foot-soldiers" to hide their actions.

Potential victims of bullying
All pupils are potential victims of bullying, however pupils who exhibit the following characteristics are more vulnerable:

- Shy

- Lacks close friends

- Has low self-esteem

- Has SEN or disability

- Is racially different

- is physically different (stammers, obese, lacking in personal hygiene)

- behaves inappropriately (irritating, provocative)

Children coming from disturbed backgrounds, in care, are young carers or from an over protective family are also more likely to be bullied.

Behaviour of victims

The tell-tale signs of bullying vary with each victim and circumstances. However the signs are a mixture of the following:

- poor attendance

- deterioration in work and concentration levels

- anxiety

- insecurity

- loneliness

- lacking friends

- low self-esteem

- negative views of themselves (ugly, failure, stupid, ashamed, too thin, obese).

Physical signs include:

- headaches

- bed-wetting

- stomach-ache

- vomiting

- fainting

- sadness

- sleeping difficulties

- self harming

Medical conditions may include:

- depression

- suicidal thoughts

- anxiety

- lacking in trust

- feeling isolated

Up to 20% of victims are also bullies themselves usually to someone younger or smaller.

Potential barriers to overcoming bullying:

- Children are ashamed / frightened to admit to being bullied.

- Children are unsure what to do or who to talk to.

- Children are worried by the consequences of speaking out.

- Children's previous experience of "telling" was negative as no-one "listened" or appeared to respond.

- Peer group pressure/collective responsibility is either a road-block or a potential solution.

- Staff unaware or unsure of real situation in their school.

- Staff unclear of procedures, actions or line responsibility.

- Staff unsure of how to help the victim or sanction the bully.

- Staff complacency. "We don't have bullying in our school."

- Staff unaware or unclear about the external help available.

- Staff acceptance that bullying is normal, inevitable, incurable, harmless and an essential part of the process of growing up and therefore unwilling to take bullying seriously.

- School lacking a positive ethos that promotes student participation and involvement.

- School does not have clear procedures for pupils, parents and staff to follow.

- School does not respond, or listen to pupils' concerns.

- Parents are unsure what to do or how to support their child.

- Parents lacking in knowledge of school's commitment or ability to tackle the problem.

- The school has an anti-bullying policy in name only. *(See Appendix 3 on page 160 for a Simple anti-bullying policy).*

Where might bullying take place in Primary Schools?

- 70% of children bullied said the bullying took place in the playground.

- 15% claimed that bullying took place in the classroom.

- 11% claimed it took place in school.

- 4% claimed it took place outside of school.

Thought for the day

More significant than anything else is the fact that 30% of victims will never tell anyone. Why?

Let us be a telling school.

Lunch Times

What sort of 'super vision' is required to make lunchtimes as productive and as peaceful as possible? For many primary schools this time during the school day is one of trials and tribulations. Many schools testify that PM in school is nearly always more challenging, behaviour wise, than AM. The **A**m **M**anaging of the morning makes way to the **P**otential **M**adness of the afternoon.

There are numerous theories put forward for why this might be, from:

   a) *There is a greater structure to the morning, to*

   b) *The children become tired in the afternoon*

   c) *The diet of the children can be full of 'E' Numbers*

   d) *The teachers are less able to cope*

   e) *The afternoon is longer without the morning breaks etc. etc.*

All the above reasons, and more, need considering and despite some schools taking steps to remove some of the above obstacles, e.g. Numeracy and or Literacy in the afternoons, Healthy eating, a break in the afternoon – peace in the classrooms still doesn't come easily. The reason, although obvious, is less easy to deal with – Lunch times can be a challenging time for the children as well as the 'super visors'.

I firmly believe if lunch times are peaceful and productive, then the afternoons can be peaceful and productive as well, becoming times for enjoyable and meaningful teaching and learning opportunities. There are many initiatives that have certainly made a difference and I propose to list some general ideas rather than detailing them.

Adult led initiatives:

1.   Engaging with the children, through structured play activities, perhaps by employing play leaders to lead play activities.

2.   Staggered lunch times, enabling the children to have more room both in and out of the dining hall.

3.   The playground divided into zones based upon different types of 'activities' e.g. quiet zone, small ball zone, another activity zone where balls are not provided etc.

4.   The employment of a sports specialist to lead activities, supported by some of the dining staff.

5.   A range of lunch time clubs: chess, football, rounders, netball, gymnastics, art, computer, reading, board games etc.

6.   The use of larger fixed apparatus to enable children to have extended play activities e.g. trim trail, soft play area.

7.   The use of larger 'moving' apparatus – e.g. chess pieces, bikes, skates etc.

8.   The installation of picnic benches.

9.   One off demonstrations – perhaps one a month e.g. Red Cross, fire brigade, police car, ambulance, library service, local clubs, guide dogs etc.

10.   Parents being involved, on a voluntary basis, to work with the children.

11.   Traditional games – 'In and out the dusty bluebells', skipping games, 'ball against the wall games' etc.

Children led initiatives:

1.   Playground Pals.

2.   Playground buddies.

3.   Equipment monitors, booking out and booking in play equipment from a Play Shed in the playground.

4.   The involvement of students from the local Secondary school – reading initiatives, play activities etc.

5.   Older pupils 'being' with younger children.

6.   Friendship Stop, where trained children wait to help children who approach them.

7.   Children leading on the playing of games.

Lunch Times to Enjoy
– the Green Card Code

A recent initiative that I have been working with schools to introduce is the Green Card Code. We have been seeking to address this question: How can the **lunch time supervisors and other support staff** reduce dramatically the incidents of negative behaviour on the play ground that can have an adverse effect on behaviour, not just during the lunch time but also during the afternoon?

Key Factors that must be considered:

1.   The supervisors must be empowered by whatever system is put into place.

2.   Any system must use the same school rules as those in place for the rest of the school day. BUT the rewards and repercussions of not following the rules must be appropriate for lunchtimes and must complement the procedures in place for the rest of the school day.

3.   The emphasis must be firmly upon a 'process of praise and not a procedure for punishment'.

4.   The dining staff must be trained to use the system.

5.   The system requires monitoring and evaluating with agreed criteria.

6.   The dining room staff must be openly supported by 'the school'.

7.   The system must be reviewed by all staff. (At least once in the term in which it's introduced).

The details of the system:
Points that must be considered.

a) **The rules** at lunch time need to be the same as the school rules:-

   a. Show good manners at all times.

   b. Follow instructions with thought and care.

   c. Care for everyone and everything.

b) **The reward system** must be agreed by the whole of the school and needs to have some reference to the fact that 'good behaviour' was being exercised during lunch time. The rewards the children receive will be in line with existing school rewards.

   Note, however, some of the rewards must have a direct bearing on lunch times - e.g.

*   sitting at a top table with an invited friend.

*   being first to receive their meal.

*   being allowed to watch an appropriate video on T.V. after they have eaten their lunch.

It is really important that each week children are recognised as excellent contributors to the positive behaviour at lunch time.

For example, a child receiving the appropriate green tickets for good behaviour could well be awarded the following:

*   1 green ticket - name read out in class in addition to receiving an appropriate memento.

*   3 green tickets - sit on top table with chosen friend.

*   5 green tickets - letter sent home and receives the Headteacher's Commendation counter-signed by a Lunch time supervisor.

- 10 green tickets – choosing a prize from the Headteacher's special cabinet.

Just as individual children have their good behaviour acknowledged the same should be done for individual classes. For example (based on the giving of 4 green tickets per day – 20 per week)

150 green tickets as a class - an appropriate video on a Friday afternoon with popcorn.

300 green tickets - a sum of money for the class to spend on some recreational resources or to give to a chosen charity or good cause.

450 green tickets - a class outing for the day to an agreed venue.

600 green tickets - invite the local newspaper in to do an article on the class with specific reference to their behaviour at lunch time.

Other 'top awards' could be a visit to the cinema or a pantomime.

A visit to a particular child friendly activity – a sports venue or a farm.

*Please note any child who has been totally unreliable in their behaviour at lunch times shouldn't automatically be invited to take part in the class rewards. BUT this must be clearly stated when the whole system is being introduced to the class and not added as an after thought.

c) **The repercussions** of not following the rules must also be agreed by the whole school and need to have some reference to the fact that repercussions for inappropriate behaviour will remain in line with existing school ones. Note however there may be some that have a direct bearing on lunch times: e.g.

- Eating lunch on their own.

- Not being allowed out to play after their dinner.

- Being sent home for lunch for a defined period of time.

- 1 red ticket - Name recorded and acknowledged by the teacher.

- 3 red tickets - Headteacher informed and a letter sent home to the parents.

- 5 red tickets – Child suspended from lunch time. (Can be time-limited).

- Further red tickets in a given month/term will result in a lunch-time ban for the child concerned.

- There needs to be a 'severe clause' in the rules for incidents such as threatening with a weapon; Physical violence towards a Lunch time supervisor. Drug abuse, Bullying of any description, continuous refusal to take heed of the rules, running out of school during the lunch time, refusal to accept a given repercussion.

d) It must be clearly demonstrated that the **school and the dining staff are working together.**

e) **Parents must be fully informed** of the system being used during the lunch break and be given the opportunity to comment on it, whether in writing or at a meeting, called to explain the new system. There should also be an open invitation for parents to visit the school to talk to someone about the new system being established.

Administering the Green Card Code system:

This is about recognising and rewarding good behaviour and signalling inappropriate behaviour.

A designated member of the teaching staff will be the manager of the scheme.
A designated lunch time supervisor will ensure the procedures are adhered to.
The focus of this system is a 'process for praise and not a procedure for punishment'.

Before introduction the whole school needs to have the process explained.

1.   It uses a green and red card system.

2.   There are twice as many green cards as red.

3.   The green cards have the three school rules on them:

•   Show good manners at all times.

•   Follow instructions with care and thought.

•   Care for everyone and everything.

4.   The red cards are identical to the green cards in terms of their wording, but are red in colour because they record incidents of bad behaviour.

5.   The total of cards should roughly equal 20% of the children staying in school during the lunch hour .i.e. 150 children - 30 cards: 20 green and 10 red.

6.   The cards are distributed amongst the dining staff ensuring that there is a 2 to 1 ratio of green to red.

7.   The green cards are for selected children who are clearly following the school rules.

8.   The red cards are for selected children who are choosing not to follow the school rules.

9.   The dining room staff must try and give out all their allocated green cards during the lunch time.

10.   The red cards should only be distributed when and if the need arises. (The red cards do not have to be given out, if no child has misbehaved)

11.   The cards will be topped up every day – enabling each supervisor to have 4 green and two red cards.

12.   An evaluation of the process will be conducted by the school against agreed criteria.

13.   The design of the cards can be found on *page 122*.

The procedure: **Green Cards:**

1.   Children seen to be following one or all of the rules can be given a green card –
       with the appropriate sections filled in.

2.   All the green cards must be given out.

3.   The green cards will be given to the children towards the end of the lunch hour for
       outstanding behaviour.

4.   After lunch-time the green cards will be given to the class teacher by the children.
       The teacher will record their names in a book. In the book is recorded: Name of child.
       Name of awarding lunch time supervisor. Name of class teacher. Date. Why child received
       the reward.

The procedure: **Red Cards.**

5.   The red cards record the children who are clearly not following the given school rules.

6.   The red cards do not have to be given out.

7.   The children who are to get the red cards are told towards the end of the lunch break.
       Please note a 'firm but friendly' warning might be given to the child who is not following
       the school rules.

8.   The red cards are given to the class teacher after the lunch break.

9.   The teacher will record the names in a book.

10.   At a 'considered time' a member of Senior Management Team will be informed about
       the child who has chosen not to follow the rule or rules during the lunch break which
       culminated in that child receiving a red card.

Please note it is important to be seen to be fair in the way the cards are distributed.
Try and share the green cards around – there will be many children who deserve them.
Be clear on the reasons you give the cards out.
Be reluctant to give the red cards out BUT when someone is clearly breaking the rules a card
should be given – the child should be informed that there is a strong possibility that they will
get a red card because ….. 'they were not showing good manner' etc.

There will be teething problems! Don't keep them to yourselves. Inform the scheme manager
or lead supervisor.

The Green Cards

- **Follow instructions with thought and care** ✓
- **Show good manners at all times** ☐
- **Care for everyone and everything** ☐

Date: _____

Name of Child: _____

Supervisor: _____

Class Teacher: _____

The Red Cards

- **Follow instructions with thought and care** ☐
- **Show good manners at all times** ✗
- **Care for everyone and everything** ☐

Date: _____

Name of Child: _____

Supervisor: _____

Class Teacher: _____

Five Different Classes

Much has been written about individual children who exhibit challenging and anti social behaviour. However, very little has been written about a phenomenon that is all too familiar for some teachers - the challenging class or group of children. I feel it is worth giving over a chapter of this book to the type of classes that, if we were honest, have ended the careers of some teachers as well as making life in school incredibly difficult. Through experience I've come across five types of classes – some good and others not so good. There is a hierarchy involved with these classes working from the downright difficult on the one hand to the mega magnificent on the other.

Different sorts of classes reflect the different sorts of behaviour of the children in the class. I have categorised classes into the following five types:

Rebellious   **Resourceful**   **Reliant**   **Reliable**   **Respectful**

The issue with the more challenging classes is what to do to help move the class forward. It is often the case with difficult classes that they have been difficult all their school career, becoming a self fulfilling disaster area. The one thing that mustn't be done is to leave them to their own devices as the class will only get worse. To make matters even more frustrating, when that class leaves the school there is often another equally difficult class waiting in the wings to take their place. These challenging classes can leave their mark on the school even in their absence. To deal with them or not to deal with them is not the question – more to the point is how to deal with them! For everyone's sake leaving them alone is not an option.

We can make a difference! No class is beyond improving and no teacher who wants help is beyond helping. In a disruptive environment hostility can come from children and occasionally teachers. Bringing about the necessary change must start with the teacher. It is their responsibility to put plans into place that will improve the situation.

Where a class is "off the wall" there needs to be **ACTION**.

A – Assertive discipline – Rules, Rewards and Repercussions

C – Consistent approach, applied throughout the class/school.

T – Take your time.

I – Involve or/ and isolate the interferers.

O – One step at a time.

N – Never give in.

One of the challenges presented to us as teachers, particularly at the more difficult end of the spectrum, is to move the class carefully and consistently through the gears - enabling bad to be better and better to be acceptable and so on. The process of making a difference is a road full of bumps, bends and brain aching bottle-necks. But, in time, with hard work, support, knowledge and experience the difficulties can be ironed out and the class of 'untouchables' can be one we begin to be proud of.

I remember, some way into my teaching career, being asked to work with a challenging class. The school advisor, when commenting on the good progress of the children, felt it was almost entirely due to the positive attitudes of teachers towards the 'class from hell' and that in itself was almost enough to move them from unreachable and unteachable to reachable as well as teachable (for most of the time).

Let's begin with the class at the 'bottom' of the pile. The class that can strike fear into the vast majority of teachers, and nearly all supply teachers. This is the Rebellious class. Rebels without a cause, apart from causing problems!!

1.   The rebellious class –

The rebellious class is almost guaranteed to present behaviour problems on a daily basis. Their reputation will go before them creating problems that can weigh heavily on the life of the school. They are a class that demands much time and effort with very little apparent reward. Their saving grace is that eventually they will be leaving! – but sadly other similar classes could well follow.

Identifying characteristics:

1.   They are a handful for all teachers, especially supply teachers. It is my experience that certain agencies will not commit their supply teachers to the schools where there are rebellious classes.

2.   They can often be boy dominated – numerically 60%+

3.   They have always been recognised as a difficult group of pupils.

4.   They demonstrate little or no respect for authority and one another.

5.   They will be dominated by a hard core of children with challenging behaviour.

6.   They will be aggressive physically as well as verbally.

7.   Their behaviour gets worse instead of improving.

8.   There is a danger that the school gives up on them and approaches adopted are more about containment and damage limitation than making real progress in terms of improving their behaviour.

9. Academically there is a low expectation of them. Equally they have a low expectation of themselves.

10. Many of the children will struggle with the basics of reading and writing.

11. There is a hard core of children in the class who come from challenging home circumstances.

12. They dislike school, often seeing it as 'The failing zone'.

Management strategies to help move the rebellious class forward:

1. The class is not the responsibility of one teacher but the whole school.

2. Such classes should be taught by teachers with lots of experience who actually want to work with them – not to 'beat them into shape' but to earn their respect by the things they are willing to say and do.

3. They should have the constant support of more than one adult. It should be a priority that the class has additional, well used and motivated support staff.

4. Targets must be set for the class as well as individual children.

5. Class targets should be realistic and supported by a well defined class reward system. These targets must be conveyed to the class and will initially be about behaviour.

6. Individual targets should run alongside the class targets. Those children at most risk must be identified first and appropriate targets given to support their special needs. (An individual questionnaire, like the one found in the R time Manual might help in identifying some of the underlying reasons for the issues within the class).

7. Other agencies must be involved, to bring added support through resources as well as expertise.

8. Teaching styles must be employed to suit the needs of the class and where possible the class should be broken down into smaller working units.

9. If feasible, reducing the number of children in the class to between 18 and 22, will help. This is not about creating a sink class but a class that can be managed more easily.

10. If possible, small withdrawal groups should be established to help with Numeracy, Literacy and Reading.

11. In addition to these 'academic' type groups there should be opportunities for the children to be involved in SEAL type groups where the emphasis should be on Motivation, Managing Feelings, Empathy, Self Awareness and Social Skills. Using programmes based around processes such as R time, Circle time, Peer Massage or small group work can produce enormous rewards in the hands of experienced practitioners.

12.   The class should be viewed as an opportunity to do something really worthwhile instead of accepting the premise that the class has always been difficult and nothing can be done with it!

13.   Recognise their hot spots and try to avoid them. For example - supply teachers can't handle them – so, try and avoid giving them 'unknown' supply teachers.

14.   Try and be creative in the way you work with them – don't be frightened to take risks with the class, but make sure the risks won't harm them physically, emotionally, intellectually or psychologically.

15.   If possible try and get the support of their parents through effective channels of communication, which could even have the effect of bringing the parents into the school.

16.   Don't be frightened to ask for extra help and be clear and specific about what the particular issues are.

17.   Ultimately you may be forced to permanently exclude a child if they continue to make teaching and learning impossible for others.

18.   It is a small steps approach but define your goals as well as the ways you intend to employ to achieve those goals.

19.   Make sure the children know you are proud of them when they achieve, as well as disappointed with them when they don't.

20.   Make sure that the Headteacher is involved as much as possible with the class. It will make a difference and I don't just mean as the ultimate deterrent!

2.   The resourceful class –

This is a class that is often described as one that is: 'Better in small doses' or 'On their own they can be ok!' They are almost Jekyll and Hyde in character – when good they are fine but when bad they are horrid. It's not always easy to know what to expect in terms of their 'teachability' but during the week the class will have its positive as well as negative moments!

Identifying characteristics:

1.   The class will be a handful for the majority of teachers, especially supply teachers.

2.   They can often have an ethos of disruption – yet at the same time they know how to behave when it suits their purpose.

3.   They tend to be a class known for a group of disruptive pupils who spoil it for the rest.

4.   They will respect some authority, yet there will be children who will have a negative approach to learning, sitting alongside those who want to learn.

5. They can manipulate teachers – playing one off against the other. Working attitudes tend to be spasmodic and often on their terms.

6. Poor relationship issues will be very apparent within the classroom. Boys tending to be aggressive and girls spiteful and cliquey.

7. Inappropriate behaviour can often be influenced by a small, yet powerful, minority.

8. Academically they can produce some very pleasing results, usually categorised by the phrase, 'It will come as no surprise'.

9. Home circumstances will vary but there is strong evidence that supports the idea that the parents are supportive, provided it suits them!

Management strategies to move the resourceful class forward.

Please note: Many of the ideas outlined above, in helping the 'Rebellious class' will also apply to the resourceful class. In addition, some of the following strategies may be of help:

1. Initially make sure the challenging children are not seated near each other and, if it is practical and can be arranged, try and place them in different classes. In one form entry schools, the latter is practically impossible unless there is a decision to vertically group.

2. Bad behaviour can be the product of the 'not fair' syndrome.

    It's not fair X can read better than I can.
    It's not fair Y has more than I have.
    It's not fair nobody ever listens to me.
    It's not fair everybody picks on me.
    It's not fair that I can't go to …..
    It's not fair. Why can't I have ……
    It's not fair they always get chosen ….
    It's not fair, no-one ever believes me.
    It's not fair. I can't help it if I can't do this stupid work.
    It's not fair I haven't got any friends.
    +++ a hundred other 'not fairs'!

3. Although the children may exhibit all of the above characteristics there will be some overriding issues that need addressing and not being able to cope with work is one of them. 'It's boring'; 'I can't do it, it's too hard'; 'Why do I have to do this stupid work?' etc. If you can identify the root causes, helping the children come to terms and deal with them can be a huge factor in helping progress. Helping them face up to their limitations and setting them on a course to do something about it can be such a rewarding process for all concerned. For example with reading: Many of the children who exhibit challenging behaviour struggle with reading.

Helping them come to terms with this and setting them on a programme that will address this problem can have such positive consequences – not least the raising of the child's self esteem. And one of the plusses of an intensive reading programme is that children can quickly see their own progress.

4.   Using programmes to promote positive relationships within the class can be very helpful. A programme which has proven to be effective is R time. This programme focuses very much on children being encouraged to get on well with others. R time should be taught once a week and each planned session lasts between 10 and 20 minutes. *Information regarding R time can be found in Appendix 5, on page 167.*

5.   Create real opportunities for some of the children to help with younger children in the school in areas such as reading, numeracy, literacy as well as general social skills such as play and practical times. Opportunities like these can be so beneficial for the child as well as the recipient.

6.   A whole school approach to a buddying system can also have enormous benefits. Giving the children opportunities to meet with other children of all ages in the school to share designated activities such as games, hobbies, literature, films, cartoons and sports etc can be really beneficial. The key to class improvement is not to isolate these children but to integrate them in non threatening ways.

7.   Bringing about change for this class might involve focussing on the few, for the sake of the many. Once again the effort is certainly worthwhile particularly when the benefits to all can be seen and felt.

3.   The reliant class –

This is a class that is almost Jean Brodie-ish in its outlook. Jean Brodie was a teacher who instead of creating independent girls created girls who became dependent on her! The girls stood out from the rest of the school as being distinctly 'Brodie'. The reliant class doesn't necessarily attach themselves to a specific teacher but tend to rely on the input from all teachers   receiving much more than they are prepared to give.

Identifying characteristics:

1.   They tend to be lacking in initiative.

2.   Their behaviour is good but the class is often accused of 'lacking in spark'.

3.   They are inclined to give the bare minimum, being satisfied with apparent mediocrity.

4.   They enjoy the attention of adults but can give little in return.

5.   They tend to be a quiet class but lack real interest.

6.   They seldom give much to the life of the school, content to arrive on time and leave with equal punctuality.

7.   They can be an 'okay' class to teach but will be frustrating when initiative is required.

8.   They will thrive on the basics but are seldom motivated to give more than the minimum required of them.

9.   Going that extra mile is a goal they will not aspire to.

10.   This is a class many teachers enjoy taking because they are compliant in the way they respond to the normal life of the school.

Management strategies to move the reliant class forward.

There can be a tendency when confronted with this type of class to coast with them. After all if you leave them alone they will certainly leave you alone. As professionals we need to be in the business of bringing the best out of our children. There is a well known saying that goes "You can lead a horse to water but you can't make it drink…..Unless you salt its oats." We need to be 'oat-salters'. But how?

There are the obvious and well tried methods, for example, target setting – both self and teacher imposed. Others worth trying include:

1.   Giving the children 'real' responsibilities, for example the children reading a story to the class. Children taking the morning and afternoon registration time.
'Loaning' some of the children to another younger class, where they can help with the learning process.

2.   Encouraging the children to do a topic on hobbies for homework. Establish an interest table in the classroom where children can bring in items that are of interest to them. This can promote a 'talk time' where the children are given responsibility for leading a discussion and sharing with the rest of the class information about an object they brought in.

3.   Having a focus on class wide reward systems that emphasises excellence in work and not just behaviour. For example, for every child who gets 100% in their Spelling, Numeracy or Science test the class will get a marble in the jar. When the class has 50 marbles in the jar the class will be rewarded by having an hour playing board games etc.

4.   Set up a class council. This would meet each month to discuss issues related to the class. The class council could have a budget and have real powers. Some of the issues discussed in class council could help to inform the school council.

5.   Invite parents into the classroom to help with the learning process. Although hearing readers is an excellent help, perhaps there can be opportunities for the volunteer parents to work alongside the teacher – supporting children in other areas of the

curriculum such as Science, Numeracy and Literacy. Hopefully the new found skills and knowledge acquired by the parents will find a way into the homes.

6.   The headteacher coming into the class and taking a lesson once each week. This can often be a source of real encouragement to the class as well as providing some valuable non contact time for the class teacher.

7.   Creating a daily diary time for the class. The children are given their own diaries. At the end of each day, in the last 10 minutes, they write down information associated with the day – and include a target for tomorrow. The teacher can be prescriptive in how the children fill the diary in. For example:

Monday: Write down something you did that pleased you today.
Work target: (Child records a work based target for Tuesday).

Tuesday: Write down something you saw that pleased you today.
Help target: Write down a way you might be of help to someone on Wednesday.

Wednesday: Write down something that you felt you learnt today.
Rule target: Write down one of the school rules that you are going to really focus on.

Thursday: Write down the name of a child who helped you today.
Relationship target: How might you encourage someone tomorrow?

Friday. Write down something that made you happy today.
Weekend Target: Tell someone at home about something that you were proud to have done during the week.

8.   Take part in an exchange with another class teacher. For example: ask another teacher to come into your class to read a story and you do the same for them.

All the above ideas are designed as a way of encouraging the children to 'box above their weight'. To help them realise they can perform well outside their comfort zones.

4.   The reliable class –

This is the sort of class that many schools will have in abundance. Known for their reliability and willingness to give of their best. Not necessarily high flyers but willing to let their kites fly. Perhaps a class best described as the Dr. Watsons to the Sherlock Holmes. Keen to learn with a real desire to find out the answers to a raft of questions. Can be relied upon to do a good job. Well liked by the school and can be easily managed by the teaching staff. Will produce a good day's work for a good days 'pay' and will certainly have their moments of inspired results. A pleasure to teach.

Identifying characteristics:

1.   Keen to please and to do well.

2.   A hard working group of children who are supportive of one another.

3.   A good class to teach because of their enthusiasm.

4.   Yet a class that will rarely surprise in terms of attainment and abilities.

5.   Solid and dependable and supportive of the school.

6.   A welcoming class, not just to other staff but to new children as well.

7.   Will be excellent representatives of the school by always coming up to the mark.

8.   Parents and carers of the children will be supportive when able to be.

9.   Will display initiative particularly when asked to.

10. Will rise to the occasions, whatever the occasions are!

11. Often involved in out of school activities both home and school based.

Management strategies to move the reliable class forward.

Why mend something that works well? The reliable class is exactly that, reliable – but there are areas where it is desirable to make more headway, for example, producing work of unexpected quality. So where do we begin?

1.   By acknowledging and affirming with the class their real strengths. How encouraging it must be for a group of children to hear they 'are a real credit to the school'.

2.   Create in them an empathetic approach to some of the areas they might like to see improved. For example an issue might be using their own initiative – that is the diagnosis so what might be the prescription? Answer: Opportunities to make real decisions – this might involve the establishment of a class council that has the responsibility of channelling class ideas to the school council.

3.   Set the class targets that might really extend their abilities both physically and mentally. In addition a class target might be along the lines of 'To enjoy learning by doing some home research on given topics'.

4.   There might be an opportunity to use the class and their welcoming and caring nature to bring a child from another class alongside them. To make that child feel welcome by supporting them in their work, and general attitude to school.

5.   A class that can be certainly used in a variety of ways but always ensure they are not over used to their detriment and that of others.

6.   You also might consider using some of the initiatives described for the **Reliant Class**.

5.   The respectful class –

A class that can be guaranteed to 'produce the goods'. Always on the ball and certainly children and adults will find it a pleasure to be with. Supportive of one another and of the whole school. A1 in every way. A class that almost manages itself!

Identifying characteristics:

1)   It is a pleasure to teach, for all teachers.

2)   As soon as you meet the class you feel at ease and relaxed.

3)   They have a well deserved reputation for being 'wonderful'.

4)   They will give more than the majority of classes in the school.

5)   Their motivation comes from a variety of sources but ultimately they are self motivated – they want to do well because they know it is important.

6)   Relationships within the class are very good and no child feels excluded.

7)   Their behaviour is always very good, setting a good example for the whole school.

8)   They can be trusted to work without direct supervision.

9)   They make a contribution to the life of the school that goes beyond their time in the school.

10)   Very supportive home background in the right sense of the word.

11)   Not often seen in many parts of the world!!! – But you know them when you find them.

12)   They usually will contain some high flyers academically, but not always.

Management strategies to move the respectful class forward.

Perhaps the ultimate class and one every teacher may aspire to work with and possibly create? I do believe that these classes can be created. Where and when they do come along enjoy them, for they not only will make you feel special but you will make them feel special too!

Be warned, however, these classes rarely happen by accident, they are often the product of hard work and the input of a succession of talented, dedicated teachers. To relax with the class is an option, but being 'lax' with them is certainly not. They are where they are, not just because of excellent teaching and teachers, but through their own desire to achieve, allied with a willingness to support each other in their learning. More of the same is the minimum requirement – what should also happen is additional input to take the class even further forward.

Thought for the day

Only the mediocre are always at their best.

Somerset Maughan
1874- 1965. English playwright, novelist and short story writer.

Supply Teachers

I know from personal experience as a supply teacher for three years that being a supply teacher is not easy, especially when you are in a school of which you have no previous knowledge. Trying to establish oneself as a member of the teaching staff is never easy particularly with the label of supply teacher hanging around one's neck. Pupils can sense weaknesses in temporary staff as soon as the teacher walks into the school. There will be times when the children feel hard done by when they have supply staff and can react in different ways, and behaving badly is one of them!

Sometimes, sadly, there isn't always the support from the permanent teachers at the school who can be jealous of the apparently more comfortable life of the supply teacher! Even Ofsted can highlight the difficulties experienced by supply teachers in a way that is not always helpful. This can be seen from the following two quotes taken at random from inspection reports:'The overuse of supply teachers has had an adverse effect on standards.' ......'One quarter of all lessons taught by supply teachers are unsatisfactory'

Sometimes the supply teachers do not help their own cause in their difficult and demanding role and hopefully the following thoughts and ideas may help both school and supply teacher alike:

The responsibility/advice for the Supply Teacher:

1. **Arrive early (if possible):** At least half an hour before the start of lessons.

    This will certainly create a favourable impression from even the most ardent of critics of the supply teacher. Be smart in appearance and efficient in your manner. Don't be frightened to ask questions however mundane they appear – it shows interest and a willingness to fit in.

    Remember the class you are teaching is not your class, but you must enforce the routines, rules, rewards and repercussions already established by the class teacher. There will be children who try to test you out, and it is part of your job to deal with them firmly and fairly.

    It is important you know about any special needs the children have in your class, especially medical needs. Behaviour difficulties should also be known in advance and, more importantly, how these are normally dealt with by the class teacher as well as the school.

    Get to the classroom before the children arrive and establish that sense of not just getting settled but belonging. If necessary move a chair or table that might help with movement around the classroom. Hopefully someone will escort you to the classroom. Asking further questions shows interest not confusion. Make sure you know what is expected of you in terms of:

a) The children coming into the classroom at the start of day.

b) The registration procedure and

c) Any whole school gatherings you need to be aware of.

2.   **Planning:** Being prepared in this area of your role is absolutely vital. As someone who spent three years on supply I always had a few 'universal' lessons up my sleeve – they came in very handy many times – not to replace the work I had been left but to supplement the times when designated planning had served its purpose. Some ideas to have with you:

a) Short stories for a variety of ages.

b) Some PSHCE activities – for example R time or Circle time.

c) Some number work that can have a fun element to it.

d) Literacy activities that can lead to the discovery of something exciting.

e) Quizzes that have their roots in fun and not just knowledge.

f) An assembly idea for the class.

g) You may have a particular strength or interest in other curriculum based areas. Create a set of lessons that will help you in working with the class.

h) Try and remember to bring some rewards that can supplement the school's way of rewarding the children – please remember no sweets or nuts or anything of a controversial nature.

i) Make sure you inform the 'powers that be in the school' about your 'box of tricks,' seeking permission to use them if the opportunity or need arises.

Usually the teacher will have left planning – fantastic! Make sure you take the time to read through this planning and follow it as closely as you can.

Resources can be an issue, particularly if they haven't been left out for you. Don't be frightened to ask both adults and children.

3.   **Support Staff:** If your class has a support assistant please use them wisely. They will certainly be an invaluable source of help and support. The support assistant will know, not only the routines, but will know the children very well. I found it very helpful to ask them to make name tags for all the children so I could call then by their given name – a very valuable thing to do when working with 'new' children.

It is important not to be over demanding with the support staff. You must remember that ultimately you are responsible for the children in the class – so use them with wisdom, respect and as valued colleagues.

4. **The daily routines:** It is your responsibility not just to deliver the curriculum but also to make sure the class is in the right place at the right time. Here a member of the support staff will be helpful. However, with or without additional support in the classroom, make sure you know the normal pattern of routines. Many schools will have the timetable for you. I found it helpful to have my own 'aide memoir' to assist me on my travels: (What do I need to know about: Assemblies. Break times. Lunch times. Playground duty. Afternoon break. Home time. After school arrangements for the children. Special appointments or visitors.)

5. **Marking:** It is part of the professional responsibility of any teacher. To ask whether to mark books, or not, shows a lack of professionalism. If you are specifically asked not to mark the work/books then that is different, but all teachers, including supply teachers must make time to mark books. The marking of work can be a profitable way to spend part of the lunch break. However, no supply teacher should leave a school without leaving their mark! And I mean on the books as well. It might mean staying after school for a short while!

6. **The Staff Room:** There will be supply teachers who never go to the staff room and some who make a point of being there at the appropriate times. I don't believe there is a hard and fast rule about going along to the staff room. Attending the staff room will have more benefits than not and it is important to make at least one significant visit even if it's only for a hot drink and hopefully a quick chat. I know from experience that not all staff rooms are welcoming places to be, but as a supply teacher you can 'welcome' others by being sociable. One of the advantages of supply teaching is you don't have to go back to the school if you aren't made welcome.

7. **Staying when the children have gone home:** If this is possible it is always worth investing in this time slot. Try and spend some time after your class has gone home to make sure that the 'classroom' is at least in as good a condition as you found it when you first entered. If you had to move furniture to accommodate the way you managed the class, return it to the original position. Complete the marking of the work and books.

   It is also extremely helpful to leave a note for the class teacher informing them of how your day went – try and make it as positive as possible. In addition note down any incidents, good or bad, that the class teacher may need to 'investigate' further. Always try and finish the written information on a positive note – teachers love to know that the class behaved well in their absence. At the end of the day thank the teacher, probably in writing, for the planning and make any comments that will be helpful for them on their return.

Finally thank the class teacher for the way you were supported, highlighting things like the lesson plans, the support staff, the helpful information left by the class teacher etc. If you do return to the school leave knowing that you will be made welcome because of the positive way in which you left.

Responsibility and advice for the school regarding the Supply Teacher: OR - How to empower/value 'The Supply Teacher'

Thought for the day

Words of thanks have a greater impact when delivered from a grateful heart.

Just as the Supply Teacher has a responsibility for the success or otherwise of their visit, so does the receiving school. Much is made about the difficulties a supply teacher can encounter and they will not be helped if the school doesn't try and support them in their very difficult role. Just as the supply teacher is walking into the unknown so the school is often the recipient of the unknown. It is vital that the Supply Teacher's involvement in the school is made as positive as possible for the sake of all concerned.

Many schools will require the support of Supply Teachers and many schools have gone down the road of appointing their own on a part time contract. Yet there will be times when the 'stranger' supply teacher is required and the following may help to make their time in the school as successful as possible:

1.   Make them feel special.

2.   Give them an achievable task.

3.   Provide them with a sense of accomplishment.

4.   Praise them for their effectiveness.

5.   Let them know that they belong and are accepted.

How?

1.   Feeling Special:

First impressions are so important and you can give the supply teacher a good impression of the school by the warmth of the welcome they receive. Someone at the school designated to meet them and acknowledge them by name. To make them feel welcome by showing them the geography of the school. Taking them into the staffroom and offering them a drink. Taking them to the classroom where they will be working and introducing them to relevant personnel. (Please note I believe this welcome should be done by an adult and not children. By using children it can place the supply teacher in a position of dependency on children and can disempower them, creating a feeling of inadequacy on the part of the supply teacher).

Give them a supply pack with helpful and relevant information which should contain the following:

- A general information sheet which should be no longer than one side of A4. Briefly taking the supply teacher through this sort of check sheet can be very helpful for all concerned.

- A simple map of the school with highlighted relevant areas – for example staff room, class room, toilets.

- A timetable for the day – times, lessons, assemblies.

- A list of the Rules, Rewards and Repercussions. The main concern of both school and the supply teacher is the ability to deliver the set curriculum; in other words, "Can I teach the class because they behave well?" Fundamental to the management of any class is knowledge of, and correct use of, the rules, rewards and repercussions.

- A list of responsibilities the school would expect the supply teacher to carry out – for example mark the work of the children, carry out the requirements left by the class teacher, carry out any additional activities deemed essential by the school. (Please note the school may feel it inappropriate for a short term supply teacher to carry out duties that involve the supervision of children outside of the normal classroom duties – for example play time duty or the taking of an assembly!)

- Make it obvious they are most welcome to use the school facilities as well as the resources.

- Show them how the photocopier works and tell them the code, if one is needed.

Make them feel part of the team. Don't throw them in at the deep end by setting them up to fail either by giving them the impossible class or withdrawing the usual support. If anything, try and go the extra mile in supporting the supply teacher.

Take them to the classroom and show them the ropes. Ensure that the designated member of staff knows the class well and how it is organised. The key to good management of the class is being aware of the issues facing the supply teacher and being able to communicate the solutions effectively. It is of very little help to inform the supply teacher that the class is challenging without offering guidance on how to deal with this situation. Equally it is very little consolation to tell the supply teacher the class has Science but you don't know where the relevant equipment is kept! To know the issues is important and to know how to resolve them is essential.

On the first occasion a member of Senior Management Team should introduce the supply teacher to the class – probably as a personal friend! When the children come into the classroom introduce the teacher in the correct way and reassure the children you will 'pop in' during the day to look at the work, emphasising the point that they should make this special guest of the school welcome. This is not about reading the riot act but making sure the children know their responsibilities.

There might even be an opportunity initially for a senior member of the teaching staff to support the new supply teacher by team teaching with them when they first start working in the school. This will enable the supply teacher to become familiar with the routines of the classroom as well as the school. It will also help the supply teacher to get to know the class in a safe and secure environment.

2.   An achievable task:

Lessons to suit: Yes we all know the supply teacher should be expected to follow the normal timetable – but sometimes it can be a recipe for dismay if not disaster. For example to ask a 'senior in age' supply teacher who has no idea about football to take a challenging class of Year 6 children for the beautiful game can cause a few expected issues. Yes I know the children will be disappointed but a sensible change of timetable can be extremely helpful for all concerned. I am not advocating wholesale changes but common sense needs to prevail in these situations.

Fundamental to the management of any class is knowledge of the rules, rewards and repercussions. I've indicated earlier that an information Sheet is very helpful for the new supply teacher; an additional set of the 3 R's is of equal value. If you adopt the 3R's recommended in Simply Behave then the following advice on a sheet of A4 will help any supply teacher and can be customised with the specifics of your school:

Simply Behave School:
Additional Support for our Supply Teacher

This is an example. Please customise the following to describe the situation at your school.

General Information: As a short term supply teacher (less than one week) you will not be expected to do playground duties or attend after school staff meetings. Neither will you be expected to lead an assembly. You are responsible for registering the children both am and pm. The class register will be delivered to your classroom. Designated children will take it to the office immediately it has been called.

Detailed lesson plans for the day, including times, have been left by the class teacher. You are required to follow them to the best of your ability. Any questions arising from the planning should be addressed to (……..insert name of contact) who is the (………………insert role) and can be found (…………..insert location). Any work done by the children must be marked in an efficient and professional way.
On the reverse side of this information sheet is a simple diagram of the school showing the key areas; and the weekly timetable for your class.

As a valued member of the school all the normal facilities and resources are at your disposal. Please ask any member of staff for help. Please note you will be introduced to your class by the Head or another Senior member of staff.

The school times are as follows:
Starting 8.55 – You will be required to collect your class from the playground.
Assemblies 9.10 – You will be required to attend every assembly apart from Wednesdays.
Morning Break 10.30. – You will escort your class to the playground and collect them at 10.45.
Lunch Break is 12.00 till 1.00 – Your Dining Room Supervisor will collect and return your children to the classroom. Please note Simply Behave School operates 'The Green Card Code System' at lunchtime and you will be required to record the names of children who receive green cards at lunch times – these are for good behaviour and the children must be congratulated accordingly. Red cards must also be recorded.
There is no afternoon break.
School finishes at 3.15 – You are responsible for dismissing your children at that time from the classroom.

At our school we use the system known as the 3 R's as part of the behaviour management strategy.

1) Rules: The school and class operates on a three rule system:
a)   Follow instructions with thought and care.
b)   Show good manners at all times.
c)   Care for everyone and everything.

2) Rewards: The school uses the acronym PRAISE as the ways of rewarding the children.
a)   P = Parents informed by letter, telephone or word of mouth.
b)   R = Rewards – for example stickers, small presents.
c)   A = Awards – for example certificates at the end of the day, golden time, supply teachers award.
d)   I = Intuitive – for example the reward fits the child.
e)   S = Specials - All children in the class have set responsibilities. A list of these is displayed in the classroom.
f)   E = Encouragement; please ensure you encourage the children regularly for their work and their behaviour and attitude.

Please note any written rewards that you give to children will be acknowledged in front of the children by the Head Teacher at the appropriate time. In addition you will be required to fill in three letters to send to the parents of children who deserve particular mention. Please copy the letters to the class teacher.

3) Repercussions:
If the children don't follow the rules then they will expect repercussions. We use a six point system that is as follows:
a)   A friendly yet firm warning.
b)   A recorded warning.
c)   A Time Out at the Time Out table for Y minutes.
d)   A Time Out in (……..insert name)'s class for Y minutes.
e)   Sent to (……..insert name) who is a member of the SMT.
f)   An internal suspension within the school.

The school will not tolerate the following:
1)   Bullying.
2)   Racist language.
3)   Swearing.
4)   Violence of any description.

In the unlikely event of this happening the child will be taken from the class by (……..insert name) who is the SMT responsible for this class.

3.   Sense of accomplishment:

Create a positive tone by building up the **incentives**. For some children the intervention of a supply teacher is just that 'an intrusion' on their well established relationship with their class teacher. They may not welcome the supply teacher and show it with behaviour that is very unhelpful. It is important that whenever possible the **children are prepared** for the supply teacher. The class teacher explains why and if possible who it will be, and the expectations of the class. If the relationship with the class teacher is good then poor behaviour is letting themselves, the school, as well as the class teacher down.

Remind the children that one of the benefits of a supply teacher is the **double reward system** the supply teacher can use – for example, instead of giving one sticker for good work the supply teacher can award two.

Supply Teacher's Award Initiative. In addition to the normal school rewards the school has a 'supply teacher award' that can ONLY be given by the supply teacher. These rewards have an important status in the school and are given by the Headteacher to those children who made a positive and significant contribution to the supply teacher's stay at the school. These merit awards can be added to the normal school system of giving rewards.

Parent letter system. The supply teacher can be given the opportunity to send three letters home on the evening of their supply day in the school, to children who have shown outstanding achievements. These letters can be 'pre-prepared' for the supply teacher who has responsibility for putting in the name of the recipient child and signing the letter.
An example follows:

Dear _____,

I have had the pleasure of teaching _____ today. They were a privilege to teach and I just wanted you to know what a credit they are to you. Along with this letter is a book token that can be spent at the local shop. Thank you for the way you support the school and the way you encourage your child.

Yours sincerely,

---

4. Praise:

Just as praise is part of the school ethos for the children then so it should be for staff, and the supply teacher is no exception. Tell them how well they are doing, especially in front of the children. Recognise and use their strengths. It is also helpful, if they are willing, to participate in a 'wider' school role – for example taking an assembly, playing the piano for song practice or assembly. Sharing some expertise that might be beneficial for a wider school audience. As the status of the supply teacher is increased so can their effectiveness in the school be.

Seek their advice. The supply teacher may have gifts and skills that can have an enormous benefit for the school. For example, they may have advanced skills when it comes to computers or music. They can have talents in craft or sports all of which may help them as well as the children in their care. Using and developing the expertise of supply teachers is a skill in itself and can only be done by making a real effort to get to know the supply teacher better.

5. Make them feel accepted and that they belong.

Being valued as a person as well as a 'performer' is something most of us value and appreciate. Encourage all the staff to make the supply teacher feel welcome. For example: Staff should know a supply teacher is coming and that they also have a name!

Establish routines based upon procedure as well as good practice helping to make the supply teacher's role and stay in the school as profitable and as pleasant as possible. Investing in people is never a waste of time and good investment will certainly reap its rewards.

Adopt a Supply Teacher. There are many good supply teachers and when you come across one try and sign them up, legally of course! If they end up becoming a regular visitor to the school please remember to invite them to staff gatherings as well as significant days in school – for example concerts, sports days or even adventure holidays where the extra support for the school and pay for the supply teacher can be most welcome.

There is no greater compliment when the school genuinely wants the supply teacher back and the supply teacher wants to return – so it's au revoir and not goodbye!

Newly Qualified Teachers: (NQTs)

Newly Qualified Teachers, or as they are sometimes known - Not Quite Trained teachers. Although I certainly wouldn't subscribe to this description there is a seed of truth in its harsh sentiment. Many Newly Qualified Teachers do not have the knowledge or resources to manage a challenging class and I have met those who have left the profession very early in their career because of the stress of trying to teach a class that doesn't want to be taught. When this extreme but not uncommon event happens the responsibility lies in three main areas:

1)   The training the NQT has received.

2)   The support the school must provide.

3)   The responsibilities of the NQT themselves.

1.   The training the NQT has received:

If you ask teachers, particularly those who have experienced really challenging classes, the one thing they would like from their class, they would respond unequivocally, 'good behaviour'. There is no doubt that well behaved classes will be a source of great encouragement to all concerned. Ask parents what they look for in a school and the answer, "Well behaved and happy children", is usually top of the list or very near the top.

So good behaviour is important – but it has been my experience that few teacher training courses come anywhere near to giving this vital ingredient of training the time, expertise and emphasis it requires. Why – because there aren't enough 'experts' around to pass on the practical knowledge. A possible solution would be for course leaders to recognise that the issue of behaviour, in terms of classroom management, could be a weakness in the training programme and to address this. Training institutions must review their training programme to ensure effective classroom management and coaching, in the area of behaviour, is given a high priority.

There needs to be a dedicated period of time devoted to this key aspect of a teacher's 'tool kit'. This time should be practical as well as theoretical. Opportunities need to be built in to visit challenging schools who have successfully addressed the issue of poor behaviour.

All too often, when a student teacher is struggling with a class, the response is to move that student to safer climes. It is also a fact that schools that have a reputation for challenging classes are either not used for placements (for one reason or another), or steps are taken to give the trainee a class that is more receptive to the learning process.

Practising teachers, with an in depth knowledge of behaviour strategies, should be brought in to work with students to develop and deliver a specific behaviour management course. It is not just about managing behaviour, it is about the ability to coach good behaviour.

The training of a teacher is based upon what a trainee teacher is expected to know, understand and be able to do in order to be awarded qualified teacher status as well as succeed as an effective teacher. These standards are organised under three broad inter-related categories:

   i. *Professional values and practice.*

This is about the attitudes and commitment expected of anyone qualifying to be a teacher – treatment of pupils and colleagues as well as effective communication with parents and carers.

   ii. *Knowledge and understanding.*

This is about being confident and authoritative in the subjects they are required to teach. In addition it is essential to understand how pupils should progress, as well as what teachers should expect them to achieve.

   iii. *Teaching.*

This is about the skills required in actually delivering lessons – planning, monitoring, assessment and classroom management.

Whilst recognising the importance of all of the above, there is an obvious need for all trainee teachers to have specific training on behaviour management and behaviour coaching. From interviewing and talking with a significant number of NQTs many expressed concern and apprehension that they may not be equipped to deal with some of the challenges around behaviour they might subsequently encounter.

2.   The support the school and the Local Authority must provide:

I believe that the receiving school has a significant part to play in helping the NQT to become trained and confident in all aspects of successful classroom management. By focussing on the vital aspects of good classroom practise the school and the NQT will have the best possible chances of a successful outcome for the probationary period. In many schools acceptable standards of behaviour are high on the agenda. The school must be confident in the knowledge that all aspects required for ensuring good behaviour management are in place, that the NQT is fully inducted into all elements of the behaviour policy and that they are able to implement this in their classroom. It is essential that good discipline is maintained. It is in the school's interest to go beyond the basic requirements of what is legally required and to invest time and effort in the induction of any NQTs – to encourage the development of valued colleagues who will be part of the school's success.

From a legal perspective the school (headteacher) has two basic responsibilities:

   i. *To make sure all newly qualified teachers receive an appropriate induction programme.*

   ii. *To make a recommendation to the local authority, based upon rigorous and fair assessment procedures, as to whether the NQT has met the induction standards.*

What are the basic requirements for the Induction Programme?

There should be a nominated, experienced, 'well trained' induction tutor.
The NQT should have no more than 90% timetable, with protected release time.
The NQT should be able to raise concerns about their induction without fear of unacceptable repercussions.
The governing body must be fully informed about the support for, and progress of, the NQT.

What is the role of the Local Authority?

The school must inform the Local Authority if an NQT joins or leaves the school.
The Local Authority must be informed if the NQT is at risk of not reaching the required standards.
The Local Authority should arrange additional work experiences (if appropriate) in support of the NQT.
The school must ensure that documentation about the NQT is available to all parties involved and must ensure that documentation is passed to other schools if the NQT moves or is transferred.
The school must ensure that all necessary documentation is presented within 10 working days of the NQT completing their induction.

Helping the NQT when problems occur:

There are a variety of reasons why an NQT might find it difficult to keep control of the children they have responsibility for teaching and managing, for example:

- The class is already considered to be a class at risk because of the behaviour of the pupils.

    Response – Only in exceptional circumstances should the NQT be given that class i.e. there is no alternative; or the NQT has an excellent track record of managing challenging behaviour.

- The NQT does not have in place an induction programme that involves the necessary observations and feedback.

    Response – In the first few weeks of teaching, ensure the NQT is observed at least twice in teaching the class, with an emphasis on basic classroom management. Prior to the observations the school should detail five basic principles related to behaviour that the NQT must follow and be observed following:

    a) *Know the rules that the class has to follow.*

    b) *Be aware that instructions and rules are different.*

    c) *Know and use the rewards and repercussions of not following the rules fairly and consistently.*

    d) *Ensure that the rules, rewards and repercussions are clearly displayed in the classroom – e.g. An A3 poster for each of the 3 R's.*

e)   *Ensure the rules are taught as well as modelled by the NQT.*

•   Despite all above being in place the class still doesn't respond to the behaviour programme.
   Response – Look at lesson planning and the management of the classroom. Examine the geography of the classroom as well as the delivery and appropriateness of the lessons for the age of the children.
   Take into account the history of the class's behaviour with other teachers.

It is a delicate line to walk between wanting to help and support the NQT whilst at the same time helping and supporting the children to ensure they have their entitlement – the best possible education. Over the years I have found it helpful to pose the question when observing a teacher working with a class: 'Would I want my own child in their care?' If the answer is 'No' then some issues need to be addressed and the school needs to take firm, constructive and sensitive action.

3.   The responsibilities of the NQTs themselves:

•   The NQT must be pro-active in their induction programme in the following ways:

i)   *By undertaking self evaluation of their progress, identifying strengths and limitations.*

ii)   *By working closely with their induction tutor.*

iii) *By keeping a record of all professional development undertaken and any monitoring and assessment reports.*

iv)   *By expressing concerns about the induction to the Induction Tutor, Head or named contact on the ISCtip. (Independent School Council Teacher Induction Panel)*

v)   *By being aware of the Induction Standards that came into force in 2003 against which their capabilities will be assessed – in particular the following in relation to behaviour.*

•   The NQT must be pro-active in ensuring they have a positive start to their career as a teacher. The following may help in your preparation:

From the Induction Standards 2003

3.3.9 They set high expectations for pupils' behaviour and establish a clear framework for classroom discipline to anticipate and manage pupils' behaviour constructively, and promote self-control and independence.

(f) Secure a standard of behaviour that enables pupils to learn, and act to pre empt and deal with inappropriate behaviour in the context of the behaviour policy of the school.

Thinking about that first day:

When Neil Armstrong first stepped on the moon on July 20th 1969 he uttered those now immortal words:'That's one small step for man, one giant leap for mankind'.
When teachers are faced with their first class it may feel like 'one giant leap'.
The heart will be beating a little faster than usual and the emotional 'swingometer' will be oscillating between excitement and anxiety.
The brain will be moving through its gears trying to recall all the advice you have been given since that day you decided to become a teacher.
This is the moment you have been waiting for.
You have arrived at the start of your future career and it matters so much that you get things right. For a stumble now could mean a fall tomorrow.
Thoughts rush into your brain:
Should I smile before Christmas?
Should I let them sit where they want to?
Should I tell them this is my first day of teaching?
Should they sit on the carpet when they come in?
Should I greet them on the playground?
Should I make name cards for them?
Should the children wear labels?
What do the children do with their coats?
Should I allow bags in the classroom?
What happens when they ask to go to the toilet?
What will they think of me?
How will they weigh me up?
What do I want them to call me?
Can I remember what I want them to call me?
Does it matter what they call me?
When should I tell the first child off?
Do I tell a child off on the first day?
How do I tell that first child off?
I wonder if they will like me? etc. etc. etc. etc. etc.

Before the first day:

Remember you have been appointed by the school because you have impressed the appointment panel with your knowledge, your professionalism, your personality and your teaching credentials. You have already established yourself as a valuable colleague – use this situation wisely.

1.   Make sure you have planned the curriculum with the children in mind. But also have more ideas up your sleeve than you need – a story, a quiz, an appropriate video, an interesting object you can talk about, a Science experiment that impresses, a spelling test – something to fall back on in case you run out of ideas.

2.   Make sure you have gone through the records of the children – being aware of any special needs – allergies, additional medical issues, a new child.

3.   Make sure you have made contact with any support staff you will be working with.

4.   Become familiar with the school and in particular the geography of your classroom.

5.   Make sure the class room is set up for the needs of your children.

6.   Make sure you are aware of the essential routines and their timings. – Assemblies, Break times, entrances and exits and so on.

On the first day:

That first day is all about **you.**
About **you** being in charge.
About **you** calling the shots.
About **you** laying down your markers.
About **you** drawing the lines and making sure the children adhere to them.
About **you** establishing yourself as a teacher first and foremost. (After all that is why you were appointed).
About **you** being in control and the children recognising and respecting that.
About **you** saying at the end of the day, "That went well, I can't wait for tomorrow".

When the above is your goal what is the route to achieving it?

There is no one single route but some of the following ideas may be helpful:

Plan for that first day thoroughly, leaving nothing to chance.

(i)   Start with how and when to welcome the children.
       If possible have the support of another adult for the first five minutes, if you feel that would be helpful. There are teachers who on that first day like the class to themselves.
       If you collect the children from the playground escort the line from the front and halt at the classroom door. Let them in one by one and greet them as they enter the class room.
       If the children come to you from the playground stand at the door, ask them to wait and greet them as they enter your room.
       Have their tables/desk with their name cards on, so you as well as the children know exactly where they are to sit when you give them their instructions.
       As the children come in, one at a time, following your directions, get them to sit on the carpet/or at their desks where they are supervised by your support person.
       Once the children are in and seated then ask your support person to leave, if that is appropriate and agreed.
       Make sure the 'disposal' of coats, bags, lunch boxes has been considered and dealt with.

(ii)   Introduce yourself and your expectations.
       Tell them the level of sound you expect during this time and then greet them with a good morning. This will require a very quiet good morning response from the class.
       Take the register in an authoritative and professional manner
       Make sure the register is taken to where it needs to go.
       Make sure the process the school has for recording lunch is followed.

Tell the children the three rules and show them displayed alongside the rewards and repercussions. Don't invite discussion.
Explain the rewards briefly yet clearly. It is helpful here to give a reward.
Explain the first three repercussions, pointing out the 'Time Out' place.

(iii)   The first lesson
        Once the parameters in which you expect the children to work have been established the first lesson can begin.
        Remember it is vital that this lesson starts with the underlining of a rule and the choice of a relevant instruction.

(iv)   As the day proceeds
        Use the behaviour plan, particularly the rewards, as frequently as is appropriate.
        At the end of the day make sure the children know you are pleased with them and why.

After the first day:

Fantastic – the first day has gone well. What next?
More of the same. Relaxing your well earned grip on the class is not an option.
Children like to feel safe in school and one of the best ways is for the teacher to be in control.
This creates the firm foundation on which to build your relationship with the children. It enables you to flex your teaching style for the mutual benefit of you and the children.
Equally you are able to demonstrate your organisational skills as well as classroom management for the good of all involved in your class.
Be known, and acknowledged, as a teacher who has good class control rather than a teacher who is controlled by the class!
Your success, and the success of the children in your care, depends on your ability to teach them well.
The root of good teaching lies not in good subject knowledge, not even in your ability to communicate effectively, but in your ability to create in your children a respect and love not just for learning but for the learning process as well.
Fundamental to good teaching and learning is a well managed and disciplined class. No class that rushes out of control comes with a ready made hand or foot-brake to re-establish control. The object is to not lose control in the first place. Prevention is certainly better and easier than cure. Be a caring teacher not a curing one!
There is of course the need to relax your grip – but it is exactly that – relaxing your hold on the class. To release your hold means to let them go – to relax means to keep your grip but in a more relaxed manner.
When and how you do that is in your hands. You will know intuitively when the class is there to be enjoyed for all the right reasons. Then and only then will your class be able to sit back and observe that, "My teacher is in charge but my teacher also respects and likes to hear from me".

CONCLUSION:

The beginning is not the end but the end is the beginning. Read the following out loud, forwards and backwards, and only then will you begin to understand:

This is the truth

If we turn things upside down

We can't be the best school in the world

I would be lying to you if I said that

Our school has a great future ahead

That we will be a fantastic school

That the way forward is clear and well defined

That our children will be healthy, be well disciplined and learn

Before anything else you must know

Our school does not deserve such things

I am convinced of this because I know the teaching profession

Laziness and lack of care are in our nature

I refuse to believe under any circumstances that

We could be a great school in the coming year

Because of everyone's contributions

The school could sink to new depths, but

There are even more surprises to come

The school has only one destiny

And whether we like it or not

This is what is real

You should know that I believe exactly the opposite. (Now read it again from the bottom up!) You may not need Simply Behave to turn your school upside down but I hope that something from the book will make a difference, not just to you but to the community you have been given the privilege and responsibility to serve.

Greg Sampson.

Section Four

The Appendices

A Behaviour Policy
based upon Simply Behave

Name of school: Simply Behave Primary School   **Date: DD/MM/YYYY**

Person responsible:

Introduction:

This behaviour policy is to determine the boundaries of acceptable and unacceptable behaviour; the hierarchy of rewards and repercussions and how they will be fairly and consistently applied at Simply Behave Primary School.

Statutory Duty of School:

The head teacher and governing body are responsible for promoting good behaviour in **Simply Behave Primary School** . The Head teacher will publicise this policy, by making it known within **Simply Behave Primary School** , and to parents, and by annually bringing it to the attention of children, parents and staff through school assemblies, the school prospectus, staff handbook and induction procedures.

Aims:

- to promote self-discipline and proper regard for authority among children.

- to encourage good behaviour and respect for others and prevent all forms of bullying among children.

- to ensure children's standard of behaviour is acceptable and does not disrupt the learning of others.

- to regulate children's conduct.

- to promote good behaviour within the school and in the wider community.

Policy into Practice:

Within **Simply Behave Primary School** certain practices will support behaviour and discipline:

a)   **The establishment of three diamond school rules, which are for all times and all circumstances:**

- Follow instructions with thought and care.

- Show good manners at all times.

- Care for everyone and everything.

At Lower Key Stage One these are worded:

- Please do as you are told.

- Please be polite.

- Please be caring.

b) **The introduction of instructions:** These are in addition to the rules and can be changed to match the activity and prevailing circumstances. Whilst children will be expected to know the school rules, they will be directly involved in establishing the instructions.

c) **Rewarding achievements:** This will be done through positive recognition of individual children or classes' achievements in good attendance and behaviour, through mentions in assembly, certificates, prizes, informing parents or carers, by employing P.R.A.I.S.E. which stands for the following:

Parents informed

Rewards in place

Awards presented

Intuitive awards that are matched to the recipient

Specials that are specially chosen to match the occasion

Encouragement of good behaviour to enable children to recognise what is

required of them

d) **Repercussions for children who choose to disregard the rules:** A series of repercussions is in place. These repercussions are hierarchical and are designed to reinforce the school rules and teach children how to follow them. All teachers and teaching assistants have the right to impose repercussions, except exclusion, which is the responsibility of the headteacher in consultation with the governors:

1. **Warning – verbal.**

2. **Warning – recorded.**

3. **Time Out in own class.**

4. **Time Out in another class (Parent informed?).**

5.　　**Sent to Senior Manager (Parent informed).**

6.　　**Internal suspension (Parent informed).**

7.　　Please note that in extreme cases **temporary or permanent exclusion** may need to be actioned in line with legal requirements.

e)　　**Strategies for supporting behaviour management:** Behaviour management techniques, assertive discipline, individual behaviour programmes, circle of friends, R time, Green Card Code.

f)　　**Strategies for promoting good behaviour:** Rules, Rewards and Repercussions will be displayed together, prominently and attractively throughout the school. Teaching about them will take place in Assemblies, PSHCE lessons etc.

g)　　**Strategies for coaching good behaviour:** Modelling excellent behaviour particularly in the area of manners. Class wide reward systems to promote, teach and reward good behaviour. Enlisting the support of parents by encouraging the use of the school rules at home. Starting every lesson with a rule and an instruction. Highlighting good behaviour when it occurs as a way of promoting positive role models amongst peers.

h)　　**Setting good habits early:** To help children establish regular attendance and good behaviour from the start, involving parents in the process.

i)　　**Early intervention:** Prompt intervention is needed where there is poor behaviour or unexplained absence, so it is clear that this will not be tolerated.

j)　　**Monitoring:** The use or rewards and repercussions are monitored at least termly according to age, ethnicity, gender, learning difficulties and disabilities.

k)　　**Identifying underlying causes of inappropriate behaviour:** Attention, anxiety, diet, habit, developmental level, uncertainty about what is expected from them, epilepsy, medication.

l)　　**Work with parents:** Support is available to those parents who may need help in the ways they handle their children's behaviour. Signposting or referral to Family Support Services such as community nurses, learning and behaviour support teams, parenting programmes as well as actioning the CAF process are all activities that are in place.

m)　　**Work with colleagues from related disciplines:** Including speech therapist, nurse, consultant paediatrician, dietician, educational psychologist on addressing any underlying causes.

n)　　**Staff development:** The school uses relevant professionals to provide in school advice and training. The staff are informed about related courses being provided by the Local Authority and other reputable training providers.

o)   **Support staff:** Supply staff are given a copy of the Behaviour Policy and the rules, rewards and repercussions available to them are explained. Lunchtime staff are trained in the use of the Green Card Code system, using the school rules, rewards and repercussions.

p)   **Sharing this policy:** This policy has been shared with all schools in our school cluster or geographical area.

The severe clause

In our behaviour plan a **severe clause** is in place so the school and children know what behaviour will not be tolerated in school. The following are incidents that will constitute the imposition of the severe clause:

·   Bullying.

·   The physical abuse of a child.

·   The physical abuse of a teacher.

·   Racial abuse of anyone in the school.

·   Being in possession of harmful drugs for their own use or for 'selling' to others.

·   Carrying a weapon such as a knife.

The following would also be considered by the school as **severe clause** incidents:

·   Swearing at a teacher.

·   Deliberately breaking or damaging school property.

·   Stealing.

·   Open defiance in carrying out one of the repercussions, for example refusing to go to the Time Out space.

·   Deliberately missing lessons by hiding in an area of the school.

·   Doing something that constitutes danger to another child, for example pulling the chair away when they are about to sit down.

·   Cheating to gain an advantage.

·   Telling lies to get others into trouble.

·   Bringing matches into school.

In consultation with the governors severe clause incidents may require putting into operation the need for exclusion – whether temporary or permanent.

Children with special needs:

We will make reasonable adjustments in the application of the behaviour policy where there are individual pupils with SEN or behavioural disabilities, and any other pupil at risk of disaffection and exclusion. The school will make special educational provision for pupils whose behaviour related learning difficulties require it.

We will plan proactively how the school's disciplinary framework should be applied to each of these pupils and ensure that all those in contact with the pupil know what has been agreed. There will be a named key person in school who knows the individual children well, has good links with home and can act as a reference point for staff when they are unsure about how to apply the disciplinary framework in the case of a particular child.

Children

Involving children will help reinforce this school behaviour policy by active involvement in the choice of instructions, anti-bullying strategies, contributing ideas through in class discussions and through class and school councils.

Parents

Simply Behave Primary School will encourage parents to support good attendance and behaviour through home-school agreements, parents' meetings and newsletters. Parents and children will be aware that the school has an equal opportunities policy and will monitor the impact of their policies and procedures on different groups (by race, gender, learning difficulty and disability).

Monitoring, Evaluation and Review

The Governing Body should review the behaviour policy every two years. It should be promoted and implemented throughout **Simply Behave Primary School**.

A simple School Attendance/Lateness Policy

At **Simply Behave Primary School** we believe it is vital that children are punctual and have good attendance to enable them to achieve their full potential both academically and socially.

Attendance:

At **Simply Behave Primary School** we will aim to achieve an attendance rate of 95%, plus. To support this Simply Behave Primary School will provide the following in an effort to maintain and improve attendance:

a) *A warm and welcoming atmosphere into which children and parents come each day.*

b) *Encouragement to the children to come to school regularly and on time.*

c) *Take the register carefully; making sure mistakes are not made.*

d) *When children are away the school will follow them up promptly by phone.*

e) *When children return from an absence they will be given a sympathetic welcome, avoiding any negative comments.*

f) *Children who find regular school attendance difficult will be given time to discuss their difficulties with the appropriate member of staff.*

g) *Parents will be fully informed about absence or lateness.*

h) *Children with 95% attendance for a term will be awarded a certificate.*

i) *Children who improve their attendance record from one term to the next will receive due recognition.*

j) *Children who receive 100% attendance during a term will be given special recognition.*

k) *Children whose attendance falls below 80% over a four week period will be monitored by having a home phone call on their first day of absence.*

l) *Class attendance figures will be posted in the reception area each week.*

m) *A half termly letter will be sent updating the parents on how the attendance and lateness drive is going.*

The school expects from pupils:

i) *That they will make every effort to attend school regularly and on time.*

ii) *When they arrive in school they will be appropriately dressed.*

The school would want the parents to:

i) *Support the school in its efforts to improve attendance and punctuality by encouraging their children to attend school.*

ii) *Contact the office (phone number provided) between 8.30 and 9.30 if their child is unable to attend school.*

iii) *Send a note to the teacher when the child returns to school.*

iv) *Make sure their child is appropriately dressed when attending school.*

v) *Make sure the child is well prepared for the school day, with what they need for the day and homework completed.*

Medical appointments

Where a child misses more than half the morning or afternoon because of medical appointments this will be recorded as "authorised absence" in the register.

Parental requests for holidays within term-time

Permission for family holidays in term time can only be granted in exceptional circumstances, where:

- the holiday is important for the well-being and cohesion of the family following serious or terminal illness, bereavement or other traumatic events.

- evidence is provided by an employer that leave cannot be accommodated during school holidays without significant consequence.

Where holidays are taken which do not fall into the "exceptional circumstances" category, these will be recorded on a child's attendance record as "unauthorised absence".

All requests for more than 10 school days' holiday leave within a 12 month period must be put in writing to the Director of Education.

When a pupil is withdrawn during term time there is disruption to the learning process and this can result in the pupil falling behind his/her group. Some parents think that this time can be made up by the school providing 'work' for the pupil to complete during the holiday period. However this does not have the desired effect since the pupils has missed out on quality teaching time.

In general terms it is our policy that it is not possible to provide your child with the work which is planned for his/her group during this period of absence. The teacher will, if possible, try to make up work that has been missed on your child's return to school. On returning to school the pupil will be encouraged to work hard to compensate for the gap in their education. This may required the completion of additional work following teaching input.

If you wish your child to continue with some school type activity while on holiday may we suggest that he/she keeps a personal diary or record of the holiday.

Punctuality/ Lateness

At Simply Behave Primary School we place a great deal of importance on the need to be punctual and to arrive in school on time.
Being on time provides a good start to the day and shows consideration for everyone else in the class and avoids repetition of instructions and teaching.
All children who arrive in school after registration will be marked late.
Any child who arrives in school after 9.30 without a parent or note will be made welcome in the school but a phone call will be made to the child's home.

Responsibility

In order for this policy to be successful every member of the school community must make attendance and lateness a high priority. We must share our enthusiasm for education, communicating its importance to pupils and all members of the school community.

Responding to non-attendance and the procedure for lateness

1.   In continued non-attendance or lateness the Education Welfare Officer will be alerted by the Headteacher and home visits will be carried out.

2.   In the most extreme circumstances a referral will be made to the local Area Attendance Advisory Group.

A Simple Anti-Bullying Policy

Rationale behind the policy:

Bullying, in any form, will not be tolerated at our school. As a "listening and telling" school we are committed to the creation of a positive and safe learning environment for all.

Bullying is present to a greater or lesser extent in all institutions. All members of the school community deserve the right to feel valued, equal and respected and be able to come to school without fear. Bullying has a serious effect on a pupil's self esteem, emotional and mental health. This prevents them from developing their full potential and can seriously affect their life chances. Our school's definition of bullying is:

> **Bullying can be defined as an abuse of power by one or more people through repeated hurtful or aggressive behaviour with the intention to cause emotional or physical harm to another person.**

It can be:

- **physical:** hitting, kicking, stealing or hiding belongings, sexual assault.

- **verbal or written:** name calling, insulting, racist remarks, offensive sexual remarks, taunting, mocking, threatening language, producing offensive graffiti.

- **Indirect/emotional:** spreading nasty stories, excluding from groups, forced joining of groups, graffiti, defacing property, displaying literature or materials of a racist, sexist or pornographic nature.

- **E-bullying:** using web pages, offensive or abusive text or email messages, sending offensive or degrading images by phone or via the internet.

Bullying takes many forms. It can be related to:

- race, religion or culture

- sexual orientation(or alleged orientation) or of a sexual or sexist nature

- disability or SEN

- appearance or health

Purpose of the policy:

*   To promote the school's aims and values.

*   To develop a positive and safe learning environment in which bullying will not be tolerated.

*   To promote inclusion, mutual respect, self-esteem and self worth in order to meet the physical, emotional and mental health needs of all members of the school community.

*   To raise the standards of behaviour and levels of achievement of all.

Guidelines for implementing policy:

*   There needs to be recognition that anyone can be a bully or a victim and that bullying can take many forms.

*   It is recognised that the Headteacher and Governing Body have a statutory responsibility for school behaviour and discipline, but that all members of the school community accept collective responsibility for the successful implementation of this policy.

*   Pupils are encouraged to report all incidents of bullying, whether they are victims or bystanders.

*   All staff will respond to student, staff or parental concerns seriously and support the agreed procedures.

Our proactive strategies include:

*   We are a listening and telling school. This is the message that will be promoted at all times and with all audiences.

*   There is an agreed collective responsibility to address any incidents of bullying observed.

*   The School Council will include bullying as an agenda item at each meeting.

*   Peer support systems for pupils will be promoted and training provided for both

*   staff and pupils.

- Parents will be encouraged to actively support the policy at parents' evenings by signing the home-school agreement and promoting the School's Behaviour Policy and Charter of Children's Rights.

- Annually the issue of bullying will be raised in order to maintain awareness of the issue through school assemblies and prominent pictorial displays and posters.

- Every opportunity to promote whole school initiatives such as an anti-bullying day, involvement in anti-bullying week, theatre productions and external speakers will be taken.

- The Governing body and SMT will monitor bullying via staff meetings, auditing proformas from pupils and parents and an annual questionnaire on bullying and school practice for pupils to complete.

- Bullying will be addressed within the PSHCE and Citizenship Curriculum.

- All staff will receive training on the identification, prevention and management of bullying. At the start of a new school year procedures for dealing with a bullying incident will be discussed at an early staff meeting. The policy will be discussed and then distributed to all new staff.

Our reactive strategies

- In the event of a bullying incident the same procedures will be followed as for all other incidents of poor behaviour (see School Behaviour policy.) Staff will gather evidence and consult with their line manager.

- In all cases details of the incident and action taken will be recorded. Parents of both the victim and the bully will be kept fully involved.

- If it is a serious incident temporary or permanent exclusion will be considered after a full review of the facts.

- Bullying incidents will be logged and monitored on a termly basis by the Head, or named member of the SMT. This information will be given to the Governing body each term as part of the Head's Report.

- This policy applies to all school staff, governors, pupils and visitors to school.

- A Governor will be nominated to have responsibility for maintaining an overview of behavioural and bullying issues.

Bullying outside school

The Headteacher has the power to respond to bullying behaviour involving pupils whilst out of school; be it on a school trip, school activity or in the community. Conduct that threatens the health and safety of pupils, staff or members of the community will not be tolerated. The Head teacher will consider the evidence available and if the claim is proven will impose sanctions in line with the school's general behaviour policy. In serious cases where an offence may have been committed the Headteacher will contact the local police.

Reviewing the policy:

The policy will be monitored and evaluated annually, involving all stakeholders. This policy is the outcome of consultation between all members of the school community (pupils, teaching and support staff, governors and parents) through questionnaires and meetings. It will be reviewed every two years.

Special Needs Related to Behaviour

Some pupils with more complex behavioural, emotional and social difficulties may fall under the definition of disabled. The definition of disability includes conduct disorders such as oppositional defiance disorder (ODD), Hyperkinetic disorders such as attention deficit disorder or attention deficit hyperactivity disorder (ADD/ADHD), and Syndromes such as Tourette's and other mental health disorders. Such disorders do not have to have been officially diagnosed in order for a pupil to be classified as disabled; the impairment simply needs to exist.

Understanding more about these disabilities:

1. ODD, or oppositional defiance disorder, is a psychiatric disorder that is characterized by two different sets of problems. These are aggressiveness and a tendency to purposefully bother and irritate others. No one knows for certain what causes it. The usual pattern is for problems to begin between ages 1 to 3years. A lot of these behaviours are normal at age 2, but in this disorder they never go away. It can run in families. If a parent is alcoholic and has been in trouble with the law, their children are almost three times as likely to have ODD. The criteria for ODD are: A pattern of negativistic, hostile, and defiant behaviour lasting at least six months during which four or more of the following are present:

- Often loses temper
- Often argues with adults
- Often actively defies or refuses to comply with adults' requests or rules
- Often deliberately annoys people
- Often blames others for his or her mistakes or misbehaviour
- Is often touchy or easily annoyed by others
- Is often angry and resentful
- Is often spiteful and vindictive

How often is "often"?

All of the above criteria include the word "often". But what exactly does that mean? Recent studies have shown that these behaviours occur to a varying degree in all children. Research has found that the "often" is best solved by the following criteria:

Has occurred at all during the last three months -

is spiteful and vindictive
blames others for his or her mistakes or misbehaviour

Occurs at least twice a week

is touchy or easily annoyed by others
loses temper
argues with adults
actively defies or refuses to comply with adults' requests or rules

Occurs at least four times a week

is angry and resentful

deliberately annoys people

2. ADHD stands for attention deficit hyperactivity disorder. A child must have exhibited at least six of the following symptoms/ attention difficulties for at least six months to an extent that is unusual for their age and level of intelligence:

- Fails to pay close attention to detail or makes careless errors during work or play.

- Fails to finish tasks or sustain attention in play activities.

- Seems not to listen to what is said to him or her.

- Fails to follow through instructions or to finish homework or other tasks (not because of confrontational behaviour or failure to understand instructions).

- Disorganised about tasks and activities.

- Avoids tasks like homework that require sustained mental effort.

- Loses things necessary for certain tasks or activities, such as pencils, books or toys.

- Easily distracted.

- Forgetful in the course of daily activities.

A child must have exhibited at least three of the following hyperactivity symptoms for at least six months to an extent that is unusual for their age and level of intelligence:

- Runs around or excessively climbs over things. (In adolescents or adults only feelings of restlessness may occur.)

- Unduly noisy in playing, or has difficulty in engaging in quiet leisure activities.

- Leaves seat in classroom or in other situations where remaining seated is expected.

- Fidgets with hands or feet or squirms on seat.

At least one of the following impulsivity symptoms must have persisted for at least six months to an extent that is unusual for their age and level of intelligence:

- Blurts out answers before the questions have been completed.

- Fails to wait in lines or await turns in games or group situations.

- Interrupts or intrudes on others, e.g. butts into others' conversations or games.

- Talks excessively without appropriate response to social restraint.

What is the likely outcome?

Many children simply outgrow ADHD. About half of those affected appear to function normally by young adulthood, but a significant number will have problems that persist into adult life. These may take the form of depression, irritability, antisocial behaviour and attention problems.

3. Asperger's Syndrome is a form of autism. Autism affects how people interact with people and the world around them. Those with Aspergers are often of above average intelligence but have difficulties interacting socially. This can lead to social isolation and eccentric behaviour.

Symptoms are varied but usually fall into the following areas:

*   The repetition of behaviours and routines.
*   An inability to develop peer relationships whether socially, emotionally or intellectually.
*   The intense preoccupation with narrow areas of interest.

There is no single best treatment package for children with Aspergers. However, the earlier the diagnosis and intervention the better. Effective treatment and support should build on the child's interests. Create and offer the child predictable and recognised schedules and routines. Teach tasks in simple and well defined steps. Help to engage and support the child in highly structured activities. Provide a clearly defined behaviour programme that reinforces and identifies how to behave.

4. Tourette's Syndrome is a neurological condition that is characterized by tics, which are repeated, involuntary, sudden movements or vocalizations. The severity of the tics can vary widely, and they range from barely noticeable to debilitating and disruptive. Common types of tics involving movements include:

> grimacing
> eye blinking
> shoulder shrugging
> head jerking
> touching the nose
> In more serious cases, touching people or things, twirling around, jumping, and even self-injurious behaviours (such as hitting oneself) may be observed.

Tics involving vocalizations include:

> repetitive throat clearing
> tongue clicking
> making strange or inappropriate noises such as yelping
> repeating others' words or phrases (termed echolalia)
> uttering swear words or racial slurs (called coprolalia, this phenomenon only occurs in about 15% of people with Tourette's Syndrome)

The symptoms of Tourette's Syndrome usually begin in childhood and generally worsen during the teen years. The severity and frequency of tics and even the type of tics can vary over time in a given individual. While the tics are considered involuntary, some people perceive the tics as urges and can learn to suppress their symptoms to a certain extent and for limited periods of time. Many, but not all, people with Tourette Syndrome suffer from other neurological and/or behavioural conditions including:

> attention deficit disorder,
> sleep disorders,
> impulsivity,
> obsessive-compulsive disorder, and
> learning disabilities

R time

Thought for the day

R time has given me friends I don't even like

Karan – aged 10

"Relationship problems require relationship solutions" by Rob Osborn (Leicestershire Anti-Bullying Strategy Manager) – October 2007.

Over the last few years much of the research to address bullying has focused around the area of relationships. We are now aware that children with secure friendships and the ability to develop positive relationships with their peers are much less likely to be bullied. The research by Craig and Pepler highlighted the need to look at the social architecture of the classroom to promote learning by supporting a student's capacity to develop healthy relationships.

A number of initiatives have developed as a result of this desire to address the issue of relationships. One programme called **R time** was developed in 2002 and can now be found in over 40 Education Authorities and was highlighted in "Bullying Today" a report by the Children's Commissioner (November 2006).

First pilot

When Leicestershire developed its first Anti-Bullying Strategy it chose to focus on Primary aged students and became the first authority to pilot R time. From a pilot in one school in 2003 R time is now successfully in place in over 200 Primary schools across the county.

What is R time

- The programme consists of a weekly lesson of 10-15 minutes length.

- Questionnaires at the start and end of the programme help to set class and individual targets, and evaluate progress.

- There are 30 sessions, for each year group from Nursery to Year 6.

Each session has five component parts:

- Random Pairing –the children work each time with a different partner until they have worked with all of the children in their group.

- Introductions – once in their pairs they greet one another with a positive statement e.g. "Hello, my name is Simeon. I'm glad that you're my partner today Sarah".

- Activities – there are 30 easily achievable short activities for each year group for the children to do with their partner.

- Plenary – the children feed back their experiences to the whole group and the teacher helps them to reflect on their learning.

- Conclusion – at the end of the session the children thank their partner and say something positive to finish.

Has R time made a difference?

Leicestershire's annual Pupil Attitude Survey has shown a significant decline amongst Primary pupils reporting that that they had been bullied since the introduction of R time. The most striking reduction has been in years 5 and 6. We believe that R time grows in impact as the work is reinforced each year from the Foundation stage.

Year Group	06/07	05/06	04/05	03/ 04	02/03	Fall of
Year 3	10.6%	18.3%	21.0%	21.1%	22.9%	50%+
Year 4	9.6%	17.6%	16.9%	17.9%	17.0%	43%
Year 5	8.2%	12.1%	11.7%	14.8%	16.2%	49%
Year 6	5.7%	7.6%	8.3%	8.8%	11.6%	50%+

R time research findings

The Leicestershire Anti-Bullying Team has evaluated the benefits of R time through the use of questionnaires each year since 2004/5 when they started with 1140 pupils from 8 Primary schools (before R time was introduced and again after 3 and 6 months). The research showed that R time had a positive impact on social inclusion, contentment in school, relationships and promoting a positive ethos. It also showed that students perceived that their school was against bullying and were increasingly willing to talk about it.

Why is R time successful?

After the initial training the programme is easy to implement and requires few resources.

It is a whole school approach and positive results quickly become apparent.

It is teacher friendly and the pupils love it.

It has no academic bias so it is accessible to pupils of all ages and abilities.

The whole programme is based on good practice and uses comparatively little curriculum time.

R time complements and supports the SEAL initiative.

SEAL

Within the Primary National Strategy the SEAL materials provides a whole school framework for explicitly promoting the social and emotional aspects of learning. These are identified as self awareness, managing feelings, motivation, empathy and social skills. They are developed through 6 whole school themes lasting half a term during which time the students have the opportunity to practice the pro-social strategies they have learned. In additional there is a smaller module over two weeks called "Say no to bullying" which is intended to be covered around Anti-Bullying Week.

A new publication **R time for SEAL** uses the R time approach to support schools in introducing and developing the materials and exploring the five social and emotional aspects of learning.

Together R time and the SEAL materials are having a dramatic impact on developing a positive school ethos in which children learn the skills to develop social skills, accepting, respectful relationships and bullying is not tolerated.

Further information

R time materials can be ordered via the R time website at www.rtime.info
SEAL materials can be downloaded from www.bandapilot.org.uk

An A - Z of Behaviour Rewards

(A host of ideas from which you might like to select a few)

There is no doubt that good behaviour contributes greatly to the learning process. It not only benefits the individual but can create that feel good factor that will encourage most to give of their best, knowing their efforts will reap the rewards of their endeavours.

For the majority knowing that good behaviour is expected is enough, however, for that to be recognised in some way is also vitally important.

The giving of rewards should be on three distinct levels:

a) The class wide rewards.

b) The small group rewards given to identifiable groups.

c) The individual rewards that are for individual children.

All three ways are necessary as well as valuable. Although the use of individual rewards will no doubt predominate it is important to ensure that class wide and group rewards are used and given equal importance and status as individual rewards.

Below is a list of ways of giving or cataloguing rewards. Although they are described as ways of giving individual children an award many of them can be adapted and presented as class and group rewards.

I have not defined them as age specific and the majority can be used to reward children of any age and either gender. What is important is that, if rewards are to be given, then they must be available to all children at the designated times. There is nothing worse for a child to be informed they are in line for a reward BUT it's not ready on time! How disappointing for the child and devaluing for the status of the reward.

A – Amusement Arcade

A cabinet display of amusement arcade type prizes e.g. key rings, cuddly toys, pencil sharpeners, glitzy pencils and pens, felt tips, toy cars, etc. etc. The prizes all have a ticket value ranging from 25 to 1000. The children are awarded tickets based upon good behaviour. The more tickets they collect, the greater the value of the prizes. Children can, of course, save up their tickets. It is important that the prizes are available when the children have gained enough tickets.

B – Being in School and On Time

Every child should aim for 100% attendance. Send a congratulatory letter home for every child who achieves a 100% attendance figure over a term. Those children who have clearly made tremendous progress with their attendance should also be rewarded. Punctuality and attendance charts can be displayed in the classroom. Older children can input the information themselves. Attendance and punctuality letters and certificates should be given regularly. Those children who get a 100% attendance over a term get a small prize. They also have their name placed into the draw for an end of year prize e.g. £40 voucher etc. All children who get 100% attendance over the year get a special trip as a group. The class with the highest attendance and punctuality gets a weekly award. (Please note good attendance can often go hand in hand with good parenting. When rewarding children for good or improved attendance it is worth considering the role parents or carers have played and reward them too).

C – Class Wide Rewards

These can be earned by the whole class and can be used effectively in the teaching of a rule or an instruction e.g. lining up sensibly. The children are told how to line up nicely and every time they do so the class is given a class wide reward termed here as a 'sound of success'. This is so called because of the sound a marble makes when being dropped into a jar, or a pebble into a pot or a ball into a bin; therefore the terms 'marble in a jar', 'penny or pebble in a pot', 'ball in a bin' etc. A designated number of counters are required as a target for the class: for example 40 counters. When the class has earned the required number they are rewarded by having a Friday afternoon video with popcorn. Please note for certain named children they can get extra counters for the class e.g. David you find lining up difficult so every time you line up nicely with the class you will earn 2 counters for the whole class! Imagine the encouragement David receives from his peers in his efforts to line up sensibly.

C – Care Candles

Caring for something or someone is one of the rules recommended in the book. If the school decides to adopt this rule then recognition for children following the rule needs to be established. The whole class can work together on this. Part of the classroom can have a large drawing of a candle displayed with its stem divided into a number of bands. As children and adults carry out acts of care these acts can be recorded on the candle. This can be done by colouring in the bands and writing on them what acts of care were being shown: for example coming into the classroom in a sensible and therefore caring manner; caring for a younger child by comforting them when they were upset etc. In this way the candle provides a visual record of the class's caring acts.

D - Diamond Time

This is a class-wide award. Each week the children in the class are entitled to 30 minutes Diamond Time in which they can choose which activity they would like to do. The children must keep the Diamond Rules all week (Show good manners at all times; Follow instructions with thought and care; Care for everyone and everything) and only lose time if they have broken one of the rules.

D - Dining Award

These awards can be associated with the green card code system. One idea is that in the dining room there is a top table that has a cloth and is nicely decorated e.g. flowers, table napkins, 'posh' knives and forks. Children can earn dining points given by dining room staff. When they have accumulated X numbers of points they can sit at the top table for a given number of days and choose a friend to be with them. The children can also be 'waited' on by a designated adult!

E - Encouragement or Empathy Medals

In the classroom you can have an empathy/encouragement easel. On this easel can be placed medals with the appropriate wording e.g. (Name of child) has encouraged (Name of child) in their reading today. When the child has received a certain number of 'medals' a letter is sent home to the parent or the child receives the appropriate certificate.

F – Friendship Flag

Once a month the children nominate a child in the class for the friendship flag award. The flag is displayed on the classroom 'flagpole' and is a constant reminder of the value children place on being a good friend. The nominations are done confidentially and if the class wishes, all children nominated can receive a flag. Awards of this nature can also be given for kindness, achieving goals, helping hands etc. A different award each month.

G - Goals Awards

Children can have their own goal net (Netball or football etc). These nets are drawn on paper and mounted in the classroom. The nets can 'catch' the children's individual goal targets (All connected with behaviour):

e.g. Tim puts his hand up to ask the teacher a question.

Priya listens to the instructions she is given.

Gurpreet plays well in the playground etc.

The child has to go along a route to the goal (Perhaps 10 steps) Once the goal has been reached the child receives an appropriate reward.

H - House Points

Some schools have adopted a whole school house system. The children become members of a given house and they retain that membership throughout their school life. Along with membership comes responsibility and the children can earn rewards and points, not for themselves, but for their house. At its best it can create the feeling of community across the whole school. If not handled well it can become divisive and too competitive.

H - Hospitality Awards

These awards can be given to those children who make others feel welcome. It may be a new child to the school but more often or not it can be the simple invitation to 'an outside' child to become an inside child – this helps to create the change from the odd ones out, to the odd ones in.

H - Helping Hands

This sort of reward is achieved by the child or children who are continually helping others. The rewards can be given for academic help as well as demonstrating the social skill of helping. It may be comforting a child who is upset. Inviting a child into a friendship group and sustaining that welcome over a period of time. It could be for helping someone who is physically hurt or bringing to the teacher's attention a child who requires some sort of help.

I – Inspiring Ingots

There will be children who have the ability to inspire others. This can often take the form of constructive leadership. Helping and supporting children in the most positive of ways. These children can be identified as natural leaders and can inspire others to achieve things that can be of a challenging nature. When this sort of leadership occurs it can be rewarded by the use of 'ingots'. A Unifix cube covered in gold wrapping paper makes an attractive substitute for the real thing! These ingots can be collected by the individual child or class and can be exchanged for prizes or appropriate rewards.

I – Instruction Ingots

As with all the rules there needs to be a reinforcement mechanism in place to help value the rule and help users to remember and follow the rule. If adopting the three rules outlined in Simply Behave it is important that the children are recognised for 'following instructions with thought and care'. The ready made ingots can be given to the children as they clearly demonstrate their desire to follow instructions as part of the rules used by the school.

I – Initiative Ingots

As above but in this instance the children can receive the ingots because they have demonstrated initiative whether it is In the classroom, around the school, in the playground or even at home. Once again the ingots can be exchanged for other awards or prizes.

I – Improvement Ingots

As above but this time the ingots are distributed for clearly defined improvements in behaviour. For example a child who finds it difficult to line up sensibly. This is pointed out to the child and a target clearly established. When the child lines up sensibly an improvement ingot is awarded that can eventually be exchanged for an appropriate award.

*Please note it is helpful if the exchange rates are clearly known by all concerned:

For example: 5 ingots = An extension of Diamond Time.

                10 ingots = A golden certificate to take home.

                15 ingots = A 'gold' medal for the child to wear.

                20 ingots = Name recorded on the 'golden wall' in the entrance hall of the school.

J – Journey Jotter

Best used with all children in the class but can be used for individual children as a way of monitoring their progress (journey) through the school day. The journey jotter is a diary type exercise. On any given page is a 'path' that is divided into a number of given segments – for example six. The segments are coloured in as the child achieves their goals:

Segment one: Arrived in school on time:

Segment two: Sat in their designated place ready for registration.

Segment three: Played sensibly during the a.m. break time.

Segment four: Showed good manners during lesson times.

Segment five: Completed their work in the given time:

Segment six: Really enjoyed their day at school.

Each day can be a variation of the previous days. The child is rewarded according to the number of segments the child colours in.

The children themselves can have a say on what sort of goals they can have in the journey jotters. If it is for individual children then often their behaviour issues will dictate the sort of contents for their journey jotter. During the day the children can have designated journey jotter time when they can colour in parts of the jotter.

K – Kindness Kites

Just as a kite mark is a sign of quality, then kindness kites displayed in the classroom can reflect the aspects of kindness demonstrated by the class. The kites can be displayed on a portion of wall or display board in the classroom (very colourful). As acts of kindness are demonstrated by adults and children in the classroom their actions are recorded on the kites:

for example – helping someone with their reading; listening when others are talking; lending someone a pencil etc. This is about setting a pattern of behaviour that is required by the class to make it a more effective place to be. In addition, it acts as an aide memoir for the children helping to establish what sort of behaviour and acts of kindness are expected.

L – Listening Labels

Some say God gave us two ears and only one mouth because He wants us to spend more time listening than talking. The 'listening labels' are exactly that, labels displayed in the classroom where the names of children can be recorded because the children have demonstrated good listening skills. These labels can be stuck on a drawn giant ear as a reminder to the children that listening is a skill that can be taught, caught as well as observed and valued.

M – Manners Medals

If one of your chosen school rules is 'Show Good Manners At all Times' then one way of reinforcing this rule is to give the children some form of recognition for showing good manners.

This can be done in many ways but a tangible option is the award of 'Manners Medals'. These can be in the form of badges, stickers, and actual medals etc that clearly show that the child has demonstrated good manners and what the good manners were: for example – opening a door; calling a child by their given name etc.

N – Noticed Notes

Recognition from an adult in the school for doing something worthwhile is almost expected and equally of value. However, children getting recognition from one's peers is more unusual. Sadly in many schools this is not catered for. The 'Noticed Notes' programme is an initiative whereby children can record the good done by others. On a 'post it note' the children can write down, or ask someone else to write down something of merit done by another child in the school or class. It may be something done on the playground, at a break time, during a lesson or on the way to and from school. These notes can then be stuck on a notice board in the classroom and can be used by the teacher in appropriate ways as further recognition for the child concerned. The note needs to have the name of the child who is being recognised, the good deed the child is seen doing and the name of the child who record the deeds:

For example: I saw Tez Bhatti comforting a child who was upset – by David Turin.

O – On the Ball

On the ball is a well known expression that refers to something or someone that is doing something that is recognised as being correct – in other words – 'spot on'.

On a wall in the classroom can be drawn a large ball or balls. The ball(s) can be rugby, football, netball, tennis, hockey, snooker etc. As the children are spotted being on the ball in terms of behaviour their names can be recorded on the ball. If you use snooker balls the different colours could indicate different aspects of behaviour:

Red = Showing Good manners.

Yellow = Following instructions with thought and care.

Green = Caring for someone or something.

Brown = Making someone feel special.

Blue = Putting someone else first.

Pink = Being very patient in a certain situation.

Black = Making sure someone is not left out.

P - Pride Points

It is important that children recognise that good behaviour is 'cool'. There are occasions when messing around is considered to be the norm and by doing so gives the children concerned some form of status within the school or classroom. Key to changing this negative form of behaviour is to establish correct behaviour as the way forward. Taking a pride in doing what is right and others recognising this in a positive way. Awarding 'Pride Points' is another way of rewarding good behaviour and publicly recognising others for doing so. The points can be awarded under the label of pride points and can be administered and recorded in a number of ways: for example Ticks in a pride point register. Acknowledgements on the pride point board. Certificates that clearly highlight the fact that a child takes pride in their behaviour.

P – Punctuality Points

This is a form of record keeping that requires very little additional administration from the teacher. The majority of schools nowadays record attendance (taking the register) electronically. Every calendar month a print out of the child's attendance can be accessed and any child who has achieved 100% 'on time' record or significantly Improved their punctuality should be given some sort of recognition. This isn't about attendance it is about being on time for school/ registration.

Q – Quiet Time Quotas

Noise levels in the classroom aren't about volume but about the appropriateness of the noise level to the activity the children are carrying out. For example 'Quiet Reading' will have a lower tolerance level to noise than, for instance, children working in groups debating an issue. What is important is that the noise level is agreed by all and should be adhered to by everyone in the class. The definition and volume associated with the activity should be clearly defined and known by the children. The voice of the teacher should nearly always be louder than that of the children.

I have found it very helpful to categorise the noise levels in terms of centimetres in Key Stage Two. For example 'We will be using for the next 15minutes 30cm voices. I will be using a 4m voice because I need to be heard at the back of the classroom'.

In Key Stage One and Foundation it is helpful to categorise sound level in terms of levels of whispers: for example quiet, medium or loud.

The children themselves can agree the noise levels and as they adhere to them there should be some recognition and reward for their efforts. This could be recorded on a 'quiet time barometer' displayed on the wall or on the children's tables/desks.

R – Respect, Relationship and Regard for others

We have the 3 R's – Reading, wRiting and aRithmetic.
This book majors on 3 more R's – Rules, Rewards and Repercussions.
Here we have 3 more R's – Respect, Relationships and Regard for others.

When we see others using respect, as a way of showing regard for others, positive relationships will thrive. It is essential that these 3 R's are not only known by the children but are valued and recognised as fundamental to the wellbeing of the school community.

You may wish to break down these awards into 3 separate parts:

i) Respect

ii) Relationships

iii) Showing regard for others.

However you choose to 'honour' the use of these 3 qualities it is very important they are recognised, rewarded and acknowledged – to encourage their use throughout the school. They make us all smile…so maybe smiley faces' badges would be an appropriate reward!

S – Stickers and Stars

Still loved and valued by children the whole world over. Interestingly you can design your own now with firms eager to supply stars and stickers to suit every need and eventuality. It is worth shopping around because even in this day and age bargains can be found.

T – Tremendous Time

There is a time when something happens in or out of school that requires very special attention. I'm talking about the special recognition an adult or child deserves for an act of outstanding merit. This sort of recognition could even get in the local or national news and it is something that requires a special award and recognition in school. This sort of award doesn't require close scrutiny to find either the event or the recipient, you will know it when you see it. But please don't let it pass without some special mention or recognition.

U – Unity Award

Bringing people together whether it is event or personality based creates a sense of community and oneness. It may not be the result of something special, unique or even of outstanding merit but it is a defining moment when the community comes together as one and is certainly something worth celebrating.

For example it can be the success of a team – sporting or otherwise.

Or an individual's effort that raises the awareness of a situation that needs addressing through a sponsored event or everyone helping in dealing with the issue.

It might be the overcoming of a challenging situation by a child that captures the imagination of peers, or indeed the whole school.

This sort of atmosphere needs to be channelled for the good of the community bringing about harmony and oneness that can help move things forward.

V – Volunteer Award

In an age that is inclined to measure one's labours and efforts in monetary terms it is often a source of amazement and inspiration when something happens that is of a purely voluntary nature. It doesn't have to be restricted to the efforts of children or adults directly involved with the school; it could be awarded in recognition to groups from outside the school who give of their time or energies voluntarily.

For example the adult who comes in regularly to hear children read.

The parent who runs an after school club.

A business that devotes time and resources to help the school with a situation.

The ex pupil who returns to school to help in a particular way.

It is important we recognise these endeavours, not because they want recognition, but to show our appreciation in a tangible way.

W – Welcoming Waves

There is nothing more comforting than feeling welcomed! That welcome smile, the offer of hospitality, the open heart type messages are often forgotten in the busy-ness of the day. This sort of award, although awarded to individuals, can be worked towards by the whole school under the umbrella of 'We are a welcoming school'. The whole school community needs to be involved from the secretary in the office, to the site services' officer in the playground, to the head in assembly, the teacher in the classroom and the child at their desk. Each one of them should be made aware of how they can make others feel welcome – from the occasional visitors, to the child who makes the daily appearance.

Some of the following ideas may help your school in creating the welcome wave!!

a) *The use of given names being used as a matter of course.*

b) *Parents made to feel welcome whatever the reason for their visit.*

c) *The expected visitor treated with courtesy and respect by the first point of contact.*

d) *Children being made welcome in the school by their peers as well as adults.*

e) *People being given time and not made to feel intruders.*

f) *Words being used wisely and not wastefully.*

g) *And so on!*

X – Excellence in Schools

Many of the previous rewards and awards are often acknowledged and given by adults, usually the teacher. The excellence in schools award can be voted on by the whole class and should be given to the child who contributes most to the class in terms of behaviour. The children are very aware of the importance of well behaved children, not just in terms of when teacher is watching but also in the unobserved adult times. This award can be a half termly award where the whole school takes part, class by class. This should be done in a secret ballot. It is important the children understand the criteria for getting this award and it is also important that the teacher, although having the power of veto, exercises it with discretion. The results can be announced in a special assembly with the nominated children receiving an appropriate reward. Whatever the reward there should be a memento to keep at home – small trophy, medal, certificate for example.

Y – Yes be yes and no be no. Making the right decisions

Daily we are confronted by choices – What should we wear? When should we leave for school? What do we do when we get to school? Who shall we play with? What shall we play? and so on. To behave in the correct way is a matter of making the right choice:

Do I listen or not?

Do I line up sensibly or in a silly way?

Am I strong enough to make the right choices?

Do I take a pride in behaving in the way the school 'demands'?

These are not, for some children, straight forward or easy choices to make and when it is clearly seen that a child is making the right decisions at the right time then this should be recognised and rewarded. This sort of achievement can often be given to the child who doesn't always find it easy to toe the party line and can be certainly used as a way of encouraging the chid to do so.

Z – Last shall be first (patience award)

The saying goes that patience is a virtue, yet how often is this virtue rewarded in schools?

The child who waits patiently in the line while other children might push and shove.

The child who waits in an undemanding way to be heard to read.

The child who lets other children enter the classroom before them because they are holding the door open.

We see it happen yet very rarely does that sort of waiting behaviour get rewarded. If we ignore that patient sort of attitude it may not prosper in the child concerned and of equal importance it will not spread to others.

Just imagine the message that could be given to other children, and in some cases adults, when a child steps up in assembly to receive an award for demonstrating patience. It, of course doesn't have to be recognised in that way, but let us recognise it in some way!

Reflective Phrases for Time Out

(The wording of these may need to be adapted to suit the needs of the children in your class. Please note if a child finds it difficult to read, having a phrase read to them a couple of times can be just as useful):

1.   'Alone we can do so little, together we can do so much'. Helen Keller.

2.   'We must all try to be the best person we can be by making the best choices and making the most of the talents we have been given.' Retton.

3.   'It takes less time to do things right than to explain why you did it wrong'. Longfellow.

4.   'Every choice you make has an end result'.

5.   'Happiness is not by chance, but by choice'. Rohn.

6.   'Time spent thinking is never wasted'.

7.   'If your thinking is right then so will your actions be'.

8.   'We were born to succeed not to fail.' Thoreau.

9.   'You cannot be lonely if you like the person you are alone with'.

10.   'Hot heads will only lose their cool'.

11.   'The snail reached the ark by not giving up'.

12.   'The most important trip you might make in your life is meeting people half way.'

13.   'We all have ability; the difference is in how we use it'.

14.   'To behave is not just a choice it is a gift to others'.

N.B. As a class teacher I found it very helpful to get the whole class of children to think about the thoughts above. This was done in a designated moment of quiet in the classroom, not as a **'repercussion'** but as a moment of reflection.

Steps to Stop Disruptive Behaviour

Rules
Principles to apply:

*   Three rules is sufficient.

*   They must be about behaviour.

*   They must be observable.

*   They must be for all times i.e. 24/7.

*   They must be for all circumstances in all situations.

*   They are different from instructions.

*   They can be used by parents/carers when the children are away from school.

Rules	Rewards	Repercussions. (hierarchy)
Follow instructions with thought and care.	Parents	1. Warning – verbal.
	Rewards	2. Warning – recorded.
Show good manners at all times.	Awards	3. Time Out in own class.
	Intuitive	4. Time Out in another class (Parent informed?)
Care for everyone and everything.	Specials	5. Sent to Senior Manager (Parent informed)
	Encouragement	6. Internal suspension (Parent informed)

Index

ST. WILLIAMS SCHOOL
ST. WILLIAMS WAY
THORPE ST. ANDREW
NORWICH NR7 0AJ